A Walk in Eden

A Guide to Inner Strength
How to Effect Positive Change in your Life-
The Story of One Man's Journey

By

Joseph Roggenbeck

authorHOUSE

1663 LIBERTY DRIVE, SUITE 200
BLOOMINGTON, INDIANA 47403
(800) 839-8640
www.authorhouse.com

A portion of the proceeds of this book will be donated to the American Cancer Society and the Lupus Foundation of America.

Cover photo - Northern lights over Prince Edward Island. Used by permission. Courtesy of Garth Arsenault, PEI Sky Shots.

Inside –Baby photo courtesy of Eric Woodruff and family

Self Portrait – Original artwork created by Joseph Roggenbeck

The Matrix, and all related media, characters and stories are copyright 1999-2003 AOL Time Warner and Village Roadshow Pictures.

The SHAWSHANK REDEMPTION by Frank Darabont
Based upon the story Rita Hayworth and Shawshank Redemption by Stephen King.
All Rights Reserved.

First published by AuthorHouse 09/24/04

ISBN: 1-4184-2888-4 (sc)
ISBN: 1-4184-2889-2 (dj)

Printed in the United States of America
Bloomington, Indiana

This book is printed on acid-free paper.

Dedication

I would like to dedicate this book to several people and events, for it, like myself, is a composition of many varied and wonderful experiences.

- ❖ To every adversity that ever struck me down, I thank you for the hidden gifts that you would offer. In each weakness I have found a strength, and in time have built a collection of integral beauty.

- ❖ To my Taoist master Mary who has disappeared into the mists of time. Thanks for the key to what I was so desperately looking for. You have forever left an impression on my soul.

- ❖ To my close friend Trina, without your encouragement, this text would not exist. Your contribution transcends words.

- ❖ To my two beautiful daughters, Jennifer and Michelle, in whose personal beauty I find two women who will change the world in their own unique ways. As a man, I saw a world. As a father, I found compassion to understand it.

- ❖ Finally, to the most influential and completely beautiful person I have ever met, my wife Cindy. If a man is the seed, then she has been the sunlight, the life giving water and the rich soil from which I have grown. I have found all of my secrets in this life by gazing into your eyes. In this lifetime, or in any other our souls would have found each other in an endless dance we may forever enjoy.

Atlas Falls

In darkness they fought
Not two but one
In strength divided
This man and his soul
Until weakness had gained
Now pinned by Fate
A defeat conceded
A victory yet claimed
The humbled warrior
In a golden sunrise
Was delivered not death—but life

JR

Foreword

Welcome to my story. I have found that at some point in our lives, we all have something that we want to say. If you discovered a gift that changed your life into a virtual dream of incredible beauty and richness beyond description, would you not wish to share that gift with every person you ever met? So my journey began. Having the human condition of being able to be in only one place at a time, I am letting this book carry my thoughts to you. My wish is to help all that seek it out. I have sought wisdom from sources that span the globe. I have studied religions, philosophies, and read manuscripts from histories greatest authors. In these I looked for answers.

"Who am I?"

"Why am I here?"

"Where do I find true happiness?" We all have questions. Do you seek your answers? My answers will not be your answers. We all perceive the universe in our own way. That's a good thing. Diversity and contrast grant us perspective. In this text, I hope to open a few doors for you. If my efforts open one door for one person, then I have succeeded. If we never meet, I wish you success in your travels. If we have, then you know the power of my convictions. Read the text, again and again. Remind yourself daily, to actively seek out your own spiritual growth. It will change you forever.

My goal is to show you how to live your life more fully today. If your religion or faith system doesn't help you live your day-to-day life, and you are not the most complete and happy individual you can be, I urge you to look deeper. In these pages lie ideas from many sources. I have selected those that are the most tangible and relevant for our daily lives. By putting it together all in one place, and tying it together with an ancient Chinese living philosophy that is know as Taoism, I hope to offer you a fresh perspective.

In this text I make no absolute claims of philosophical or religious preference. I believe there is enough room in the world for all possibilities of spiritual guidance to coexist.

What I focus on is how to effect permanent change in your daily life. By introducing simple yet powerful concepts, my goal is to provide you the tools to change your perspective.

I use Taoism as my theme, a single thread that is woven through all of the elements of this text. I believe you will find it does not conflict with any of your ideals. In fact you will conversely be surprised how the concepts fit seamlessly in your own experiences and ideas. It is necessary for me to define these in the first chapters, so that we may have a common understanding in our travels through this book. Be patient as you progress through this early material. Think of it as a climb to the top of a roller coaster. Things really accelerate once we get going!

My writing style is unique and I hope that you find it refreshing. My goal is to paint a picture and play a melody for you in words simultaneously and in a form that keeps drawing you forward. Trust me, you have not traveled to where we are going. When the text has finished, I think you will be pleasantly surprised that indeed, I have taken you to a form of the biblical Eden.

Many of these concepts you may have already heard. Most do not conflict with any structured religion. It will be the perspective we view them from that becomes so intriguing. Keep an open mind. I hope to hear some doors opening. Think of these pages as a gentle walk with a friend, through a garden of infinite beauty. Come, walk with me, there is much for us to see!

Table of Contents

Insight

We feel incomplete in many ways, most of our lives. Nothing ever seems to fill the void inside our hearts. Man alone does not have the understanding to live in isolation. A universe exists out there. It is full of new concepts, ideas, and experiences just waiting to happen. By limiting ourselves to being only "safe" and continuing to take the well-trodden path that has only led us in circles, our isolation has left us stagnated. We breathe, but we do not live. We see, but we have no vision. The roads of man are all well known. If we follow those that have come before us, we will arrive exactly at the same destination that they did. The destinations of these roads have been mapped out and followed by many. We all know where they will lead us. If we wish to find our own place in this life, our own true destinations must be reached by following our own trails.

But we fear the unknown. It is unexplored, and unpredictable. If our lives have become so mundane that we ignore our own internal calling, what more can we really hope for in this life? To truly leave our mark in this existence, we must overcome our fears, challenge ourselves, and dare to find what lies down that path untraveled. When our final day arrives as we all know it surely will, what will we have left behind for those who follow?

It all must begin with awareness. We reach a point in our lives where our own motivations and self-interests are not enough to satisfy our needs; something is lacking, and we begin our search for what is missing. But we find that our happiness can be oh so elusive. I would like to share with you a little known secret.

You have to feel a part of something bigger than yourself.

By connecting into a faith, religion, or philosophy, it helps you gain perspective. Whatever you find that contains your answers, it must provide you a greater understanding of your universe, your life, and most importantly, yourself. Only by seeing the whole picture can we really be at peace with ourselves.

Some like a structured religion, it tells them what to do. The dogma and rituals feel safe; in time they like the feeling of the familiarity. It can be comfortable to them. The social club atmosphere gives them companionship. The actual gathering of people for a common cause or idea is very powerful. The weekly reinforcement is a solid part of their regime. It is by far the first choice of the world's population. It is the source of contentment for many from their birth to their grave.

But for some of us, our questions remain unanswered. We find conflicts in these religions that cannot be resolved within the confines of their beliefs. So where do we go? Some choose to go out on their own, to live within their own ideas and thoughts. If you find all your answers this way, you are a great sage indeed! Isolation can be a good tool. It gives us time to reflect. Just do not use it too long. Remember, balance is achieved through perspective. By considering and experiencing many things, we can make a more complete solution. A good carpenter has many tools that he uses to create a masterpiece. Each has its limitations. It is important to use your tools wisely.

Did you ever feel like you were missing something in your life? Have you ever felt there is a bigger picture that you just are not seeing? When you unlock your mind, and understand truly how our lives can work in perfect harmony with any occurrence, it is like the blind man who now can see. A whole new world exists for you to explore! Your isolation is stripped and you are carried away in a current of understanding. The common needs of everyday man are an empty promise, and you burst through the darkness into a blazing light and warmth that you just knew existed in this life, somewhere waiting for you. You will ask yourself, "How did I not see it all before?" It is literally,

The world within your world.

"What can this mean?" you ask. "I know what I see and what I feel. How could I have been missing something so obvious?" Remember these thoughts as we travel through the pages of this book. For now, let me just say that there is a duality, a parallel and coexisting presence that surrounds us continually. Many of our spiritual teachers experience it in varying degrees. Anyone is capable of experiencing it.

There have been times in your own life that you have crossed over into its beauty, and felt its presence in your heart. Without proper understanding, and with the burden of living a complicated human existence though, they were fleeting moments, and only left us with memories of passing joy and happiness as we passed back again into the reality of our daily lives.

Think right now of a time, a moment, or a memory of an event where everything in the world seemed absolutely to make sense, and in that moment of your intense joy, you felt complete and part of it all. Perhaps it was an emotionally charged event where you were so full of intense feelings of love that your whole entire self was at one with your surroundings. Was this not one of the most powerful and satisfying moments in your life? In that moment, you were experiencing, the world within your world. How you desperately must find it once again! I know exactly what that feeling is like. As my own development progressed in my search for it, I have found the secret in how to find it, that you may live that memory as a reality for the rest of your life. Though this may sound unlikely right now, be patient in your understanding and keep an open mind as we progress in the text. I assure you, you will be returning to that feeling of overwhelming happiness again in your life. This time though, you will understand how to stay, nurture, and build it in your heart to where you literally are experiencing an incredible alternate reality of complete calmness, understanding and satisfaction in all you do. It all begins with a description of an ancient concept known to the Chinese as the "Tao" (pronounced "Dow").

But what is this Tao? In this chapter, I will attempt to describe the indescribable. It has been attempted by many, but ultimately the Tao is a spirit that must be felt in your heart.

There is an old story of the ten blind men and the elephant. Each was asked to touch the elephant and describe what it was they were feeling. The first man felt the elephant's hide and told how rough and hard it was. The second man felt the elephant's ears and mentioned that they were very smooth like silk. The third blind man felt the trunk and thought the animal was very agile. Eventually, all ten men had ten different opinions of what they had experienced.

A description of the Tao has many similarities. For each of us, a different experience awaits. One thing is for certain and universal though. After feeling the Tao in your heart, and knowing where to look for it, you will endlessly seek it out forever for yourself. The Tao is as vast as our ability to comprehend it.

There comes a time in each of our lives, where we really begin to question our existence. Our goals, our careers, our priorities all come into question. Is this what I really want? Why am I not happy? With a deeper analysis though, the central point focuses on one most important word—*contentment*. It seems our ability to handle all of life's crazy turns and bumps in the road, never are really reconciled within our hearts, and our desires lead us farther down the darkened path. While these may appear as negative events in our lives, they can be a catalyst for us to change. The choice is ours. With the narrow perspective we have been taught, most choose to suffer, and hope for a better tomorrow. There seems to be in life, one of four paths that are open to us.

One, we are fortunate, lucky or just blessed with a steady and relatively uneventful existence. Though we hit a few rocks in the road, it is a pretty easy ride. No life changing events. No catastrophic challenges. While many of the masses ride this road to their grave, there is an emptiness in their lives that cannot be described in easy terms. Having never been forced into a corner by a severe and life challenging adversity, mainstream ideas and thinking are all that is required to complete their daily tasks, until life has run its course. While these are normal good people, there is a void in their development as complete individuals.

> "Far better it is to dare mighty things, to win glorious triumphs even though checkered by failure, than to rank with those poor spirits who neither enjoy nor suffer much because they live in the gray twilight that knows neither victory nor defeat."
>
> *Theodore Roosevelt*

> "I went to the woods because I wished to live deliberately, to front only the essential facts of life, and see if I could not learn what it had to teach, and not, when I came to die, discover that I had not lived."
>
> *Henry David Thoreau*

If we approach our lives as a baseball player just trying not to strike out, we are content with an achievable task. When the game is over though, we were just another average player, on another average list. But the man who swung for the fence every time, enjoys his victories however few they may have been. He knows at the end of his day that he did his best, and makes no excuses on his third strike. He has given it his all.

Two, there are those who have been given the challenges of life, and fail. They hold on to a sorrow, give up, turn to all manner of addictions and self-destructive behavior, and lose the chance to take their adversity and forge it into a tool to make themselves stronger. We see them every day, and I carry much sympathy for the turmoil in their souls. While every day is a chance to begin making a positive change in their lives and become stronger than they were before, no action is taken, and some slip even farther from the happiness they had once known.

Three, there are those who have been given some Herculean tasks to survive. A painful marriage, loss of loved ones, physical handicaps, or just a mind that sees a strange world around them and never stops looking for an answer to who they are, what life is supposed to be, and how it can all make sense to them so that they can truly fulfill their paths and destinations. Not all challenges are obvious. Though some of those around us appear to have normal lives, they may actually be carrying weights far beyond your imagination. Even if their problems are imagined or magnified in their minds, remember this is reality to them and thus can be just as painful as the real thing.

But these people are fighters. They apply themselves with what resources they have, and try and change their existence. In the struggle to survive, they uncover a hidden door within their soul, and discover a beauty and power within themselves that is the rare gift few of our fellow travelers in life have come to know. They never will view life the same way again. Once unfolded, their new-found wings carry them to heights unseen. Their deep and intangible warmth you feel in them is a gift that fulfills their lives with intensity richer than any man of wealth can claim. While adversity may have wounded them, they are the victors, standing over the remains of their fears.

Four, the most rare of all, we may have found in our journey the most unique of life's travelers. These are the angels, the heroes, and the amazing people who completely rock our senses. Nothing alters their happiness. They move through life changing our lives in ways untold. They are the example of who we can be, if we really want to. They are the model and the inspiration for our need to change. We cannot look at our own lives the same way again. While those that meet this description are truly exceptional, they do exist. How wonderful to have found one! Once you finish this book, you will have an insight into how they have become who they are. With proper change and attitude, you may even draw them toward you, or even become one yourself. The attraction is all part of the natural cycle of the Tao. The ability to join them and share in their beauty exists in every day. We just have to make the conscious effort to "become."

"Love is the difficult realization that something other than oneself is real."

Iris Murdoch

"Love is, above all, the gift of oneself."

Jean Anouilh

As I studied the writings and teachings left for us to improve our perspectives, and with it our lives, it became increasingly clear to me that all humans suffer deeply in their lives, and I was not alone. It was time to look deeply into my soul and find just who really lived there. Words cannot describe what I eventually uncovered. It was brilliance beyond all I could imagine. The transformation was miraculous, complete, and utterly permanent. Once released, it has expanded out, changing not just my own life, but all that cross my path. It all began by looking inside myself.

There was a point in my past where my future seemed very dark indeed. As time passed, I continued to fail at conquering all of the challenges that were piling up around me. Life had come to a standstill for me. In search of some understanding to my problems, that no stone remain unturned, I eventually studied Far Eastern Chinese philosophies. I wanted the answers to my questions of life and my place in it. This was no small task. It took everything I had, and required a great deal more character than I originally had begun with. Persistence and Fortitude were the horses that drew my chariot forward. I could no longer afford to accept the world at face value. There was a force hidden within me, and I was determined to uncover it at all costs. Failure was not an option. It felt it had become a battle for my moral soul.

Eventually I uncovered what I had been looking for. It is a "living philosophy" originating from China called Taoism. The basic concept pictures our existence as a balance—that good and bad, happy and sad, dark and light, all balance each other. As humans, we want only the good things. But the ancient Chinese believe there is good in every bad, and bad in every good. We just need the wisdom to see it and understand it in our lives and accept what we cannot control. With this perspective, life is constantly balanced and complete. Nothing is ever lacking. Giving yourself away and never being the center of your own desires you can find true happiness. I can honestly tell you it will literally change your life! It has taken years of retraining my understanding, but I have achieved peacefulness that I once only dreamed possible. When I stopped looking for what I had been missing in my life, I inadvertently uncovered it! By never focusing on my desires or self-interests, I actually have found it all.

After using these techniques for several years, I felt very comfortable with how effectively they had changed my life. I was in control now. I was happy every day. No matter what it brought to me, I learned to accept and appreciate it. But as fate would have it, I would need to call my horses into battle yet one more time.

The time for the real test had arrived. I was diagnosed with a 5-inch by 3-inch cancer tumor in my chest. "OK," I told myself, "this is it. If I can get through this with my Taoist approach, then truly I have found the secret to life."

Using this technique I walked through my cancer with so much strength, I totally shocked everyone I met! I quietly met with my co-workers, told them I would see them again in maybe six months, smiled and shook their hands and waved "so long." They could not believe what they saw! I smiled and laughed at my chemo sessions, no hair, sunken eyes and all. I talked quietly for hours with my fellow patients. We passed the time peacefully. We shared our fears and held each other's hands. I totally looked past the disease and only tried to be positive and show those around me a different view of life.

The response was unbelievable! It never ceases to amaze me that people don't think that they can have options or choices on how they live their lives! We make those choices every day when we get up in the morning. I tell myself, "I am going to have a great day!" It all starts with attitude. When I lay down at night, I try to think of one thing during my day that was beautiful. Sometimes it is hard. Some days there is just not much to smile about. But the more I try, there is always something. The smile from a stranger, a flower in a field, or a sunset that for just that one special moment was like no other; most days there are so many things I have to stop counting so I can get some sleep!

With all of the modern medicines and crazy chemicals running through my blood, the pills, the self-injections and finally radiation therapy, it was with incredible control that I never actually even thought about the disease. I figured the more I thought about it, the more control I was giving it over me. Though my body had a battle to win, I concentrated on my world around me, and not on myself. When the dust settled, I calmly moved forward with my life again. Once more, the difference in the battle was one of perspective and attitude. The test was over.

In studying different concepts, I had to keep an open mind. As a child I firmly believed that there was a common spirit that passed through all things, both animate and inanimate; the trees, the morning sky, the wind whispering in my ear, and the warm sunshine that wrapped itself around me. Here I felt safe and always at home and true to myself. I knew somehow that there was a connection to it all that I was missing. All of these things were quietly, gently calling from just outside my senses. Though I always felt I was a part of it all somehow, my shadow was my only tangible companion.

As I grew older, the complications of everyday life and adulthood swept these feelings aside; life had become too busy to spend time thinking about these things. Only after I had stripped myself of all of the armor that I had acquired in handling my life for so many years, was I able to feel them all calling me back, just as they had when I was a child. It was my ability to strip myself of all my desires and return to a simple balanced life that allowed me to return to the happiness of my youth and finally understand how life, the universe, and my place in it were all intrinsically tied together.

In studying Taoism, the Chinese also believe in a force that encompasses every object in the universe. It also tells us that there is a balance to this system that has been in place since the beginning of time. All of life must grow, live and pass beyond. But that is not the end. We continue on in various forms in an endless cosmic recycling. They tell us that by understanding all of the good and bad in life, we can achieve a greater understanding of how this all works and make our daily lives happier by concentrating on helping others and not concerning ourselves with our own trivialities. Wow! Quite a tall order for just another every day guy, wouldn't you say? I didn't think I could get that far, but I have, and so much farther.

I would like to explain something very important at this time. When I began reading about the concept of Taoism, it was like *revisiting* a book I had already read! All of the concepts were thoughts that I had carried in my heart, but when I actually sat down and saw them in print, it was like coming home! I had no adjusting, convincing or radical life styles to change. I actually had been following the path to my answers all along! My point is, when you seek your spiritual answers in life, you will *know* when you have arrived. I knew immediately that I had found what I had been looking for, and you will too. It will all happen at the right time, for the right reason. It always does. The interesting thing about studying the Tao is that the ancient Chinese claim that they just gave it a name. It has forever existed in the very form it is now. There are no rituals. There are no social clubs. No one is asking for money. A very simple connection between you and all that exists. It is simplicity beyond imagination.

The First Door

For us to stop our lives of confusion and pain, it is necessary to look at other concepts and ideas that we have never been exposed to. For any decision in our lives to be made with confidence, we must look at all of the facts, and then decide which the best path for us to take is. If you have unanswered questions about your life, your purpose, and your understanding of the universe, you have come to the right place. Be patient as we traverse and unveil an ancient living philosophy. Your objectivity here will be rewarded. While it is out of the scope of this book to cover this topic in its entirety, I offer you all that is necessary to unlock your mind. As I have promised, you have not been to where we are going.

Languages in history have common difficult translations. What one group of people develop to convey ideas, seldom are transposed identically by other races, in other locations, across the spans of time. With this basic understanding, our "Western" ideas and developed cultures rarely have common parallels with our "Eastern" neighbors. While the United States was once thought to be the melting pot of cultures, the result is one very different than that of the East. While we are comfortable with our own traditions, let us look to ancient China and learn some history, some new words, and perhaps a new outlook on our lives.

Let us begin with an English translation of the Chinese word "*Tao.*" Known simply as "path," or "the way," it is basically indefinable. It must be experienced to be understood. The Tao is all that surrounds and flows through all things, both living and non-living. It is an invisible force that pervades every object seen or unseen, in every part of the universe. It does so with a perfect synchronicity that flows through our daily lives in an unfolding and often unseen wonder. All of life is a beautiful, complex, and choreographed series of non-coincidences. Because of our own desires and lack of understanding, we have become removed from this natural dance, thus we miss out on the opportunity to really understand our existence and how to move within it. From the raising of our continent up from the ocean floor, to the wind that blows across our face, all things interact with an independent appearance, but with an invisible thread that weaves it all together.

The form known as the Tao has no beginning. It has no ending. It is timeless—before the earth, before our solar system, and before space itself. Is the universe the largest entity that exists? It may not be. Remember—an open mind sees what all others cannot. While we cannot see it in conventional terms, we see, hear, feel and taste the Tao in all of its manifestations.

Picture a beautiful mountain scene. Look closer. We see the trees, one by one. Yet there are hundreds of varieties. Within each branch are millions of intricate patterns of indescribable richness. Within this are the unique patterns of the bark, with roots of equal yet hidden complexity. We touch the branch and feel the bark, the contrast of the snow tingles our fingers as brown needles gently float to the ground. There is a unique scent that brings satisfaction as we take it all in. It all has an order to it that we simply cannot measure or describe. This is "*Li*"—a translation meaning "organic pattern." This can be used to describe intricate patterns in nature. The endless flowing of wind swept curves in the sand, or the fascinating mosaic of a spider's web. There is no explanation in their patterns, nor is one needed. They merely are, and our appreciation of their beauty is the manifestation of the Tao to our senses.

We now merely have looked at the tree externally. Internally, it is exchanging our life giving oxygen. It is providing food for creatures yet unseen, providing shade to all that enter, and protecting the countryside from periods of wind that would wear the earth away if left unchecked. There is much more to examine here. If we were to accelerate time and watch this scene, we would witness the pine cone, the seed enriched, drop to the ground and form its own roots. A small sapling emerges, weak, yet supple. It bends in the wind, and returns to climb as it holds its arms out to take in the life giving sun. The parent tree has withered, now a home to millions of insects, which feed from its decay. The parent crashes as one day its strength finally leaves it. The sound startles a hawk, which leaps from his perch. The rabbit scurries to safety. The hawk's shadow paints the ground in a sharp fleeting pattern that contrasts the snow, now a memory that vanishes with his departure. The echo of the hawk's screech returns off of the canyon walls, and the moment vanishes. The Tao is all things in motion, in constant interaction and in perfect order, in patterns man cannot conceive.

Daylight fades and the moon casts its gentle glow through the landscape. Intricate shadows shape the darkness in shades of twilight now owned by the night sky. The scene fades as we move silently back, and let nature hold itself; a peace that man seldom ever can know.

It is with utmost humility that we must give ourselves to this force, that we may be one with it and truly experience life.

In harmony with the Tao,
The sky is clear and beautiful.
The earth is strong and content,
All creatures prosper together.
Following the Tao,
In perfect harmony,
The cycle of life replays.

When man interferes with the Tao,
The sky is darkened,
The earth cannot sustain,
The balance is unsteady,
And creatures disappear.

The Master views all things with perspective,
So he can understand the whole.
His constant practice is humility.
He doesn't glitter like a jewel,
But becomes one with the earth,

As common as dust.

Chapter 39 of the Tao Te Ching

We have witnessed here the cycle of nature, yet have only studied but one tree in simplistic understanding. Now expand this process to the stream, the snow, the clouds and the wind, which also make up this picture. The complexity and interaction is studied by science, catalogued and processed. Every molecule is analyzed, that life may be discovered and understood. While the scientist crawls in the dirt, let us stand miles back and take in the beauty before us. We see that life, nature, and our own flesh and blood are subject to a wonderful cycle that repeats itself, with a force that cannot be found by science. This is the Tao. While man studies a part, he overlooks the whole. By thinking beyond himself, he begins to understand the manifestations that surround him, and finds a new order that he has until this day in his life, totally overlooked. This is *"the world within your world."* It cannot be explained in common terms, but is instead experienced. While nature is not the only source to observe the Tao, the close connection is ideal for our purpose of discussion here.

With this brief but colorful depiction, can you imagine the overwhelming intensity with which a man can absorb all that goes around him, in perfect understanding, with an awareness that defies description? With proper actions, he now becomes part of the movie of life, a film about himself, not removed merely as an observer. My own observations show that man spends much of his life watching his own actions and chasing distractions. To truly understand all that we are, we must stop our personal distractions and desires which hold us back from sitting down and watching the movie of the universe which is always quietly playing before us. Once you begin this basic level of awareness, you no longer will be content to be the observer. It draws you in so deeply, that your consciousness reaches a level of critical mass, and an internal door in your mind bursts open to reveal an alternate reality that you have felt at times, but never knew how to reach. No longer do you watch the movie, but walk quietly within it! This is the beginning of understanding the Tao. Thoreau eloquently portrays this image in the following quote from Walden.

> "Be a Columbus to whole new continents and worlds within you, opening new channels, not of trade, but of thought."
>
> *Henry David Thoreau*

Thinking outside of conventional terms is the trademark and the strength of the open mind. The greatest minds in history were those that chose to think and look differently at their surroundings. Instead of following conventional thought, they followed the unmarked trails to their answers. Though we commonly estimate ourselves as free and independent, do not be so sure you are not a slave to conventionality.

In our formal education in life, many gaps of knowledge need to be filled, that we may grow and truly mature in our understanding of who we are. Teachings from our schools rarely are allowed to reflect religions and philosophies. While this supports the separation of Church and State, it also removes the bridge for our youth to cross over as they begin the search for their own independence and identity, that they may begin trying on new ideas for themselves. Only the family unit is left to supply religious education and moral values. While we teach as we have been taught, we seldom look at all of the great teachings that we may speak with confidence from our convictions. Let us study a man whose legend speaks to us from one of histories most intriguing documents. While the history of the concept remains uncertain, the wisdom it provides for us is without question.

A Brief History Lesson

An ancient traveler in China around 604 BC named Lao Tzu (Alternate names: Lao Tse, Lao si, Lao Tan, Laozi) is believed to be the founder of Taoism. Chinese history often claims that Lao Tzu was a pen name for a man known as Li Erh, the head librarian of the imperial archives at Luoyang, under the direction of King Wu of Zhou. Lao Tzu was able to study history, the sciences, literature and philosophy. Here Lao Tzu developed a deep understanding of the universe, man, and his role within it. Like many great religious leaders and philosophers both before and after him, Lao Tzu sought the pure Truth that he felt inside himself. In his heart he could feel it there. Man's own self-interests and complicated lifestyles kept him from discovering this pureness. Lao Tzu felt this same pureness in all of his surroundings, and wrote of how all things are interrelated and connected. There was a great cycle not only to life which man can see, but also in all things, most of which man could not see. When a man follows the cycles instead of resisting them, he finds the contentment he so desperately has been seeking.

When the political scene became unsteady, Lao Tzu decided to leave civilization behind. He left Luoyang and headed to an unknown destination beyond the famed Great Wall. Before leaving the gate at the Great Wall, a guard at the gate was totally in awe of Lao Tzu's wisdom. When told that he would not be returning, the guard asked Lao Tzu to write down his philosophical teachings of the Tao. While complying with the guard's request, Lao Tzu compiled a short eighty-one chapter summary of his ideas in a most profound, yet brief format of approximately five thousand characters.

This book is known as the *Tao Te Ching*, (Pronounced "Dow Day Jing," meaning "The Book of the Way") which has survived over 2,500 years. It is believed to have consisted of two sections, known as the Tao Ching and the Te Ching. The first was comprised of thirty-seven chapters, the second of forty-four chapters. These were most likely written on bamboo strips, or slats, which were bound together to form two scrolls. These would then be "closed" like a vertical blind, and the characters would flow from one slat to the next. The Tao Te Ching is the second most translated publication in the world next to the Bible. Approximately forty-two versions exist in English alone.

It is also believed that Lao Tzu was a mythical character. There is some evidence that many of his ideas had been in circulation and had been compiled by a group of scholars. In either case, it really makes no difference whatsoever. The Tao has been in place long before the Earth itself. The concept remains, and has stood the test of time. Again, the reader is reminded that this is neither a religion nor a formalized doctrine. It is merely the first recorded recognition of a deep and encompassing perspective that was embodied in print for the first time in the Tao Te Ching.

Along with Buddhism and Confucianism, Taoism became one of the three great teachings of ancient China. With the advent of Communism, religious freedoms have been repressed, and many of the ancient traditions have long since faded. Tradition and ritual however are a deep part of the Chinese culture, and all three remain alive and well today. Many Western people have begun to rediscover these concepts, and incorporate them within their own existing religious beliefs.

In this book I refer to the philosophical basis of Taoism. With any major concept, various splinter interpretations and religions have been born, and thus have spread from the original Tao Te Ching. The Chinese used these concepts to impart a Taoist influence on art, science, healing and various other aspects of human existence. Let us keep to the basics. Simple concepts are all that are needed to understand Taoism. While great philosophers interpret every aspect of this history and reflect on every minor point in excruciating detail, let us leave them to their destinations and us to ours. We merely seek to have a deeper meaning to our lives, and find a level of happiness that may sustain us.

This leads us now to one of the most fun and tangible concepts of Taoism! It is known as *"P'U"* translated to mean "Uncarved Block." Man works tirelessly to form his own self-image. In this process, he accumulates many characteristics that do not serve him well. With no other method of understanding and no better way to reach his goals (which invariably are empty and fleeting), a rather despondent and sad compilation of utter complexity and disappointment often is the result. Though we have moments of happiness, our existence is always perceived as one of unfulfilled destinies.

If a man can strip himself of his desires, reduce his demands on life, and live in a simplistic approach, he returns to his core, the Uncarved Block. In the Uncarved Block he finds that all he has sought from outside himself has forever existed within. There is no need to try and reshape himself to a form that he chases in his mind. When we sit down and look honestly within ourselves by turning away our worldly desires, we see our own natural form within us—the Uncarved Block.

Once we recognize this idea as the truth, a sudden miraculous synchronicity arrives instantly at our disposal! We no longer force our lives in directions that are simply not meant for us. Instead, we gently follow the river of life in its utter pureness and natural direction, being one with it now in stark contrast to our former self who constantly caused his own sorrow and difficulty by seeking his own desires. The reward is one of immense beauty that must be experienced to fully comprehend. Naturally and with no effort on our part, life will bring us all that was ever meant for us to own. There is no need to struggle, desire, or long for an experience we feel we have been lacking. It will flow to you through the river of life. It always has! In our busy misplaced lives, these opportunities have drifted by us thousands of times! Our inability to see them for what they were, allowed them to pass us by. In returning to the Uncarved Block, we remove the mirror that we have held before us, our own narrow view of life and our own self-interests are all we have been able to see. Beyond that mirror we have been carrying around, lays a universe that only the open heart may explore. Here is where the Uncarved Block roams freely.

This leads us to another important concept known as "*Wu Wei*," which is translated to mean "life without effort." While there are many ways to walk through life, a Taoist looks carefully at what comes naturally to him, and quietly and without effort, follows where life leads him. There is no preconceived goal or prize, thus he is rewarded by living a life with no disappointments. Wherever he is, it is the right place to be. This is the concept of Wu Wei.

Difficulty can be avoided,
Before it has arrived.
Being brittle, things are readily broken.
Being small, things are easily scattered.
Control the future,
While it is still the present.
A tree as great as a man's reach springs from a tiny seedling.
A journey of a thousand miles begins with a single step.

Success is found in proper timing.
Timing is found by watching the Tao.
Knowing when to act,
The master is never out of step.

Therefore the sage takes action,
By letting things take their course.
The end he sees in his mind.
Thus he holds success before he begins.
In wanting nothing,
The sage has it all.

He lives only to show men how to live,
And find truth and pureness in their hearts.
His happiness bursts forth, covering the earth.
A wind as subtle as a whisper,
With the strength of a storm.

A natural force,
Now one with the Tao.

Here Lao Tzu points out the obvious, which is easy to recognize in print, yet disappears in the fog of our daily lives. By recognizing trouble before it begins, he appears to have done little, but has actually done a great deal. This is known as action without effort. In his humbleness, he is able to see the answer while others miss the question, their arrogance drowning out the voice of reason. In not trying so hard to be successful, he succeeds. While it appears he is not working hard, he has acted before anything can happen, and is thus rewarded by control and contentment in his life. It is literally living life without effort.

This is a very foreign concept to our Western society, where pushing for a regimented success formula has been laid out for us, a myth that would hold the key to our happiness. But as some of our culture has found, there is an emptiness in climbing the "success ladder" which has been dictated to us. We stumble in confusion when we find that the key that was promised, opens no doors for us, and has held us back from those that were once unlocked. While we struggle to reach these fleeting goals, time passes us by. Moments that could have been passed in tranquility are replaced by turmoil or perhaps at best, mediocrity.

In studying the concept of Wu Wei, a man may indeed become successful, by following where life leads him. In his measured success, he makes decisions based on his instincts, and lives honorably. Many things may have drifted by for him to take, or perhaps very few have come his way. He makes do with either one. This is his secret, and is his key to happiness. The man who arrives at this same point and pushes exhaustingly towards the elusive corporate ladder finds bitterness and despair. Knowing the balance of our goals and desires is the great secret. Not all things are meant to be. Learning to accept what is offered is a reward beyond all riches.

In understanding Wu Wei, we find that by letting things take their natural course, we arrive at our proper destination, with the key of contentment in our pocket. Pushing in directions that show us great resistance, we find discontentment, and find that through all of our efforts, we may arrive at the same destination, but much later and with our lives in disarray. The distinction here is one of proper action and timing. While we appear to be doing little, practicing Wu Wei actually makes life look easy.

Watch the pole-vaulter as she runs in calculated step. Though her pace seems casual, she sees her goal, and with firm concentration places her pole at the exact spot. While instinctively throwing her body upward, a natural grace and beauty is observed as she appears to clear the bar effortlessly. It seems so easy to watch, but just try and perform this same task yourself!

Here we see the perfect example of Wu Wei; action without doing. Another competitor with greater power attempts to overcome the bar with aggression and brute strength, and fails. He may have all of the individual skills, but does not relax his mind and coordinate the proper balance of his actions. Success is found with timing, conserved energy and patience. In applying this to our daily lives, we find we actually accomplish more, with less effort! We merely have to become more objective, and find that the way to our goal may not always be the straight path. Having fun on the way is a reward known to the great sages. It is a key for you to use, if you have the strength to take it. With an open mind, you will capture the essence of the Tao. To be able to hold it is wisdom beyond all.

Let us jump for a moment to a movie I am sure most of you have all seen—*Star Wars*. The exciting plot of Luke Skywalker who discovers he has a strange power that has lain dormant within him known as "the Force." As he raises his awareness of this power, he becomes stronger and more confident. As he progresses in his training, suddenly new events come his way. With every challenge passed, the bar is raised, and he rises to clear it. He is joined by others of his kind, and faces a confrontation with the "Dark Side," an evil opposing force that rivals his own. While he resists, it is obvious even to himself that there is an element of this "Dark Side" within him. Through his own introspection, he is faced with a choice, either "the Force" or the "Dark Side."

George Lucas has eloquently played out his own training of Taoist study, and has drawn us in to a fun movie that personifies the most fundamental aspects of this Eastern philosophy. "The Force" is the sage's true understanding of his world around him. It is strengthened by his own selfless action and his detachment from his own desires. Once experienced, it really has a power that is greater than all that you have known thus far in your life. George Lucas found this for himself and allowed it to play out for us in one of the most successful movies ever made. It also incidentally launched a career for him that has enjoyed remarkable success. Is this mere coincidence? I don't think so. His ability to understand the Tao and follow its wisdom has brought him success both professionally and personally.

In our study of Star Wars, we see the most basic teaching of Taoism: Yin and Yang. "The Force" represents Yang. Yang represents everything about the world that is bright, evident, aggressive, active, warm, hard, strong and masculine. The "Dark Side" represents Yin. Yin is all that is dark, hidden, cool, passive, yielding, calm, soft, receptive and feminine. Together they coexist is various degrees, in all that we know. One cannot be found without the other. In the famous Taoist symbol, you can see the seed of each, hidden within the other. They coexist peacefully when each is recognized and allowed to function on its own accord. Peace is broken when there is an imbalance in the Tao.

The symbol shows the most basic function of Taoism, the Great Cycle. Here we begin to assemble fragments of knowledge we own into a new picture, one that will lead beyond mere knowledge. This is simply understood as Awareness. The key concept here is one of recognizing the Great Cycle—the Earth that is formed, the animals that evolve, and the passing of life into death. We have been aware of these basic teachings, but they haven't *taught* us anything. If we expand this concept beyond mere known science, there is a cycle to *everything*. Man's destructive behavior, his desires that continually lead him into a darkened destiny, are the balance to pure love, a call from a friend, and the look into the eyes of a loved one, who confirms their affection for you in a moment of complete joy.

This cycle affects all of us simultaneously and in equal proportion. Eternally present, it continues to flow to all things. It carries in it the wisdom and truth known to all Taoists; there is a balance and reason to everything in our lives. Here we find that time is cyclical, not linear as our Western society has modeled. A Taoist smiles at this limited view. Her understanding looks far beyond the brief recorded history of man. When we view the entire universe as a cycle, we begin to see the "Big Picture" of just how humble our existence is. There never is an end, just an incredible force that pervades every object, every moment in our lives, with a synchronicity beyond that which we have previously overlooked.

When we understand that beyond every blue sky lays a blackened darkness, and within that darkness lay worlds unknown, even more beautiful than our own, awareness appears that shows us perspective. All is not what it seems. The Taoist accepts all because she knows it is part of the Great Cycle, and celebrates every moment no matter if it were strong Yin or Yang, thus her mind is clear, and confusion cannot enter. Life is all a balance, and she never allows herself to be drawn away from her detached objectivity.

I can best describe it for you this way. I have a family, wife, children, home, and a very demanding career. Although these things are all a part of my life, they are not my *entire* life. I keep them safe, with what resources I have. When events occur out of my control, I accept them as part of the Great Cycle. I know there is good within the bad, and wait patiently for its manifestation. With proper action, I induce no troubles into my existence. Wu Wei in action; though appearing to live in simple happiness effortlessly, I achieve it by not causing additional problems in my life. I act when necessary, with no more or less action than is needed. No worries—ever. I also temper this when "good" things appear to me, for there is equal Yin within them as well.

I watch my day from a vantage point as one would from a camera high above me at all times. I see myself performing these actions while working like a normal person to the average eye, but in actuality I am calmly detached while my eye also follows the Tao, the cycles, and the millions of events that are occurring simultaneously all about me. The secret is to view life from a third person perspective. The first person view as we have been taught is the only option we have ever known. We have been trained to respond to our environment in a reactionary way that would continually bring only the good things into our lives. This is pure Yang, and holds an imbalance that is proven in our reaction to life's more darkened events. If I view my life from the third person view, I have the objectivity to evaluate all things before I decide if and how to react. The result is more control. My emotions are in the back seat, not the driver's seat. This keeps me centered and in control, because all things are kept in perspective with the "Big Picture" constantly in my minds eye. With no desires and no self interests, I am free to care for all that surrounds me with no detraction from myself. Conversely, all of the positive elements I encourage in my day are seeds thrown to the wind. They grow and mature, bringing happiness back into my life in ways untold. This is my happiness, and now your understanding.

This is the great balance of Yin and Yang, in their endless cycle, in their natural form and purpose. By not contradicting the cycles, I live in a peaceful balance. When faced with cancer, heart attacks and my own mortality, I smiled and said to no one in particular, "And so it is."

If I have found this much strength, then it also waits for you; the power of perspective and the discipline to follow it to its fruition can be more fulfilling than anything you have ever known. Those that wander in life have never experienced this concept. When you feel and see a man in his unhappy predicaments, it does not take long for even the most novice of Taoists to see where the cycle is unbalanced. Remember to watch your own life continually for proper balance, for this is the secret to contentment.

We know beauty only because we have seen ugliness.
We recognize good because we have known evil.

Thus wealth buys poverty.
Difficult and easy complement each other.
Long and short compete for the eye;
High and low balance the land;
Before and after continue on forever.

The master goes about, appearing to do nothing.
She says little, which says much.

Events appear, and she lets them pass.
Her stance is firm yet yielding.
When the day is over, she has more
Than the man who has worked tirelessly.
Work is done, and then forgotten.
Forever her actions continue on
As endless as ocean waves.

Chapter 2 of the Tao Te Ching

Now that we have an understanding of the basic concept of Taoism, allow me to put your life and all of your questions in some different perspectives. When we have finished, I think you will find that life has taken on a new image, and from this new vantage point, you will never feel quite the same again. Living this way is richly rewarding and peaceful. If you have been wondering what is missing in your life, follow me deeper, as we walk into a role of new understanding. Before the credits of our lives begin to play, let us watch the movie of our life, not as spectators, but as participants. The story is yours to direct.

Joseph Roggenbeck

In God We Trust

Let us talk about God now. I feel a cumulative tension from all of my readers suddenly! We are very defensive of our beliefs, are we not? Entire races have been wiped out, in countless wars, over countless Gods, and our perceptions of them. Faith is an amazingly powerful gift. It allows us to endure the unimaginable. No wonder we defend it so fiercely!

Our traditions have handed down to us some very powerful belief systems. They exist in many forms, under many names in many places all around our planet. They have evolved, strengthened, declined and provided mankind with an intangible, invisible strength. We use this strength to fill an empty place in our hearts. This occurs from our lack of understanding. Man has not been shown the entire picture at his birth. He seeks through an entire lifetime, to fit all the pieces together, that the universe and his world and his existence all should come together in perfect order. That answer is hidden out there somewhere, we know it; we feel it in our hearts, and we push on for resolution.

All of this is understood and allowed for in looking at our Gods. Let me point out something very obvious yet crucial to a new understanding here. A God, in any form, is a man-made image that is formed from our imperfect minds. Our perceptions of it are limited to our own prejudiced views, cultures and histories. The religions of the world are equivalent to the ten blind men touching various areas of the elephant. Each of them comes away with a different experience to relate. The important connection to make here is one of vision. We cannot see a God. Neither can the blind man see the elephant. Our race has become involved in ridiculous battles over who is "correct" in their assessment of the elephant. How silly! In all of our wisdom and cultural development over thousands of years, we cannot see this for ourselves? If I could stop the entire human race for just five minutes, this would be my message that all would hear.

Now that I have cracked open a door of curiosity in you, I would like to open it a little wider now. All faith, all religions, and every thought we have ever held in trying to comprehend God, are merely our manifestations of the great entity that exists in every object, creature, culture and evolution that has and ever will exist. This is the wisdom that Lao Tzu describes for us in the Tao Te Ching. He does not claim to have the answer about God. He merely tells us where to find it!

Look, and nothing can be seen – it has no form.
Listen, and nothing can be heard – it has no sound.
Grasp it, and it cannot be held – it is elusive as the wind.

From above it does not appear bright.
From below it does not appear dark.
It returns to nothingness,
Yet appears everywhere.
It is greater than our ability to comprehend it.
Yet is as simple as a stone.

You hold it in your arms,
Only to find it is holding you.
If you understand the Tao,
You will know yourself.
The two are born within each other.
Know this
And the universe is yours.

Chapter Fourteen of the Tao Te Ching

Taoism is purely a description of the beauty and power and unending vastness that is the collective cohesive oneness that is know to Taoists merely as the "Truth." It is called the Truth because it is pure. It accompanies us from birth to grave in so many millions of manifestations, that no man can really encompass its entire wisdom in one lifetime. It has existed long before Lao Tzu named it Tao. He tells us this. It will continue on long after man gives up looking for it. In trying to label it and dress it up for human consumption, we distort its inherent pureness and power.

Within the depths of eternity
The mystery came forth
Giving birth to the ten thousand things.
It is seen as brilliant. It is seen as darkness.
Eternally balanced,
Man sees its image,
But not the form.
Infinite and ever present,
It is the mother of the universe.
For lack of a better name,
It is known as the Tao.

It flows through the universe,
And returns instantaneously
Creating all things.
Impartial and silent
The Tao is universal.

The universe holds the Earth,
Earth holds man,
Man is humbled,
And thus knows the Tao.
The cycle completes its course.

Man follows the earth,
Earth follows Heaven,
The Heavens follow the Tao.
The Tao follows only itself.

Chapter 25 of the Tao Te Ching

I have known thousands of people in my life. All have held varying degrees of faith in countless systems in their attempt to understand God and comfort their lives. The results I have witnessed have been very incomplete. In our attempt to travel to the land of the greatness of God, we have tried to take with us, the baggage of human existence. In trying to fly to the heights of its beauty, we fall vainly to our humble beginnings. To understand this bigger picture of God, Tao, or any other word that you have for it, you must first become something that you are not. All of your desires must be left behind, every one of them. You cannot want anything for yourself, not even your next breath. You must release your will that clings so intensely to this world and all of its misleading conceptions. To truly learn to fly, we must leave the weight of our human desires behind us. You must become deeply compassionate for every object, every manifestation of the beauty that is woven within every thing we see, taste, feel and hear. All of our senses are not sufficient to take in all that is happening around us, in every second of every day, in every place in the world, the universe, simultaneously, and in perfect order.

In understanding a Taoist viewpoint of the world, he lives merely to pass beyond all of the trivialities of human existence and see and feel the truth that is the pure power of the source of all things. I can assure you one thing that I have found to be an absolute and unequivocal truth. Whether you call it Taoism, or any other imperfect name, and no matter what faith, culture, or belief you hold, a true understanding of the perfection that we seek desperately to understand cannot be attained without committing your entire soul and every ounce of strength you have to become the most complete human you can be.

This is the task every Taoist takes on for himself. He gives himself unselfishly to the world in every way he can, that he may further understand, feel and become one with the incredible miracle of truth which Lao Tzu labeled "Tao" for us. Once you see even a glimpse of the truth that it holds, there is no other pursuit for him to hold. It is pure love, pure truth, and the answer to every question he has ever had. It is the complete understanding of all that is. Human needs no longer hold an attraction for him. There is nothing he wants from this world, and so, he paradoxically has everything. Even my words to describe this are woefully inadequate. I can only offer you the inspiration to seek it out for yourself. It is a gift only you can give to yourself. Once opened, it is the only one you will ever desire.

The result of this comprehension is the purity you find in every true Taoist you will ever meet. But because the challenge is so great, they are very few and far between. You will find them characters of absolute incredible personal strength. They are truly compassionate and honest to their very core. In their subtle yet brilliant humbleness, they will overpower your senses. It is the strength of their pureness in an intense and almost electrical field of energy that they emanate that draws continually your attention to them. A master of the Tao is a servant to the entire world. In meeting them, understand that they have become a purer form of the manifestation that is the Tao. Compared to our own earthbound selves, we are humbled. A closer inspection of their behavior can be puzzling to the casual observer. They look like average people, and do nothing particularly obvious in their actions, but yet they are so interesting and open! There never seems to be enough time to talk to them. The discussions could go on forever. Their warmness and compassion truly are an extension of the Tao, the warmth you feel is the jewel that they carry always in their heart. When you feel this and experience it for yourself, it may trigger a reaction within you to deeply wonder what this person has, and how you may one day emulate it for yourself. If you possess the strength and character, it is as readily attainable for you as it was for her. A Taoist has placed no limits on herself, therefore she is prepared to take on any task that comes her way. There are no limits to who you can be, except those that you place on yourself.

From my own personal viewpoint, it makes no difference what we call ourselves, or what God we serve. As long as we understand that we should not be blind to the vastness of the truth, in its absolute purest form, we may join the unbelievably small rank of sages who have gone before us, and be that special one unique human that we know and feel in our hearts to be. Not many of us feel this call. Fewer yet pursue it. My hope is that one day you will own the jewel of the Tao, and know these words for the truth yourself. Until that time, continue to wonder. It is the beginning of thought that leads us down the road of understanding. I feel many of you on the path. No man can understand your inner drive to become, except those that have gone before.

The ancient Chinese called a person who reached this state of mind, "Enlightened One." I cannot describe it for you in words. Words are merely an imperfect image of what I feel in my spirit. When you arrive in this place, you will know the truth I describe for yourself. All of your work, your desires, and your struggles to understand your world will be left forever far below. Eden has truly opened its doors for you here. Welcome home.

Joseph Roggenbeck

One Woman

I am the mirror, that the beauty you see
exists in you as you see it in me.
The desires you carry, in time will find
the dust of your past as you leave them behind.

Every angel has always held her own wings.
She merely uncovers them with the knowledge
that all of existence sings
through the songbird that bursts forth from within her soul
and in that one moment, she has found her role.

In the strength of this one woman
an entire race may find
the beauty of the Tao
that is the fabric of her mind.

JR

A Video in Words

So now that we have a concept, an idea, and a rough sketch in our minds of an age-old idea on how life, the universe and all within it function together, I would like to do something very unique at this point. I have brought props, pictures and sounds with me to illustrate to you what the Tao is and where to find it. You have stored all of the necessary images in your imagination. I want to pull them out and show them to you in a different context than when they were stored there. Picture them intricately in your mind as you read this. Think of it as one of those motivating videos you have seen where the pictures change, a complete new snapshot and image is flashed one after the other, all being displayed while a very captivating rhythm plays.

These images are all designed to capture the essence of the Tao in your minds. Once you see them, you will recognize the patterns in your daily travels, and begin to understand the world within your world.

❖ The Atlantic Ocean, the soft sea breeze touches your hair, as you taste the salty spray on your lips. In the distance, two whales swimming side by side, the foam trailing in their wake as they call out to each other. The sun glistens off of their backs as they continue their endless leaping progression. They submerge, and the waves conceal their last position, the moment vanishes. Fade out.

❖ A small back porch, simple yet tidy. Evening falls quietly. A simple set of chimes whispers softly, calling out to the breeze that gently dances with it. The breeze retreats into the darkness, and its friend the chime waits patiently for its return. Fade out.

❖ A cold winter snowscape. A single oak tree sits waiting for you in a field. Grasping its few treasures of last years gown, several leaves chatter in the wind, a companion to the cold wind that tingles your nose as the chill on your face contrasts with the warm shirt that has begun to form from your travels. A tall black shadow dances lightly in contrast to the bright snow that is rejoicing from the sun's morning visit. The snow crunches sharply in contrast to the shifting crystals that dance across the outer hardened crust as you break through with each step. You glance behind to see the stark contrast of your footsteps that have marked your entrance into winters glistening white blanket. Fade out.

❖ A young child sitting in a high chair, her mother patiently stares, pleading compliance for the completion of the next spoonful of dinner. The dog waiting patiently for the next morsel to fall. The clock waiting patiently for the second hand to wave on the next minute that longs to pass. The baby laughs suddenly, the mother smiles, and the next minute has crossed over into the open door of the past. Fade out.

❖ A busy day outside a corporate office building. A small woman tries unsuccessfully to walk with grace as the vast package collection she is carrying endlessly squirms from her grip, leaping to join gravity in its relentless mission of attraction. A stranger gently retrieves them with a wordless smile. Her face whispers a silent "Thank you!" by its gentle color change, and her own smile awakes to meet his. The steady stream of bodies flow around the island of the two who have shared a fleeting moment. The camera rapidly fades back, and only the motion of the crowd below is left. Fade out.

How did you like that? Were those not all simple things of sound, taste, touch and natural beauty, all happening simultaneously in different places of the world, all of which contain some magical element to them? That is the beauty of the Tao! It has leapt onto these pages for you so that you may see just one glimpse of its intense encompassing mystery. Can you imagine waking every day, looking for these and finding them in your entire day, filling your senses with the beauty and understanding of how they interact, gracefully, seamlessly with the universe that quietly and softly whispers the Tao into all of life, all of the objects we hear, see, touch and taste? Life *can* be like that! I know. I live it every day, and so can you. The world within your world; we have caught glimpses, felt it on occasion, but no one has ever shown it to you or defined it!

A retraining of our senses and priorities is in order to stay here, in this mystical plane where everything makes sense, and happiness is a constant flowing stream for you to play in. In life so far, we have been led in Western thinking to "take the checkered flag." We look for happiness in objects like new houses, new cars and new exciting relationships. Exotic vacations surely hold all the happiness we need, do they not? They may, but what about when the vacation ends? Fifteen years of marriage have replaced our exciting courtships. Our car now needs a new transmission. The house has become a financial burden. Time has an interesting affect on all that we know. Our bodies no longer look like they once did. Nor do they function like the ones we had in our youth, do they? Our natural tendencies lean continually to keep renewing these desires, to get another shot at holding the first place trophy. So we replace, retire, sell and sometimes even destroy our present in search of some big day at the racetrack where everything will be fun again.

The lesson of the Tao is so much different than the reality I have just acknowledged for you. We no longer try to force our lives into patterns that just don't fit our needs. We recognize the fact that rain does not ruin a perfect day; it brings with it a fresh clean scent that cleanses the earth, provides living nourishment for all of the plants, fills the oceans and captivates us with its intricate songs and rhythms as it dances on our window sills. It refocuses our attention to the small things in life. It is the collection of all of these minute events that make up our days. If we can find happiness and solitude in the smallest of events, the darkest rain clouds, the most solitary moments we experience, then truly we will look forward to each and every day and understand that no matter how it turns out, the correct thing happened for the right reason.

We no longer need to win races to be happy. The walk to the racetrack has brought us an entire day of entertainment in all of the new things we have decided to take time out from our day and acknowledge. If we never get a chance to drive a racecar again, there is nothing lost. Life is about attitude and perception. Changing these will surely change your life. I have much more to show you. Come walk with me, into another part of my garden.

Wisdom in the Shadows - A Closer Look

In my description of the Tao thus far, I have painted for you some very positive, simple, yet intriguing pictures, and in your mind they will stand out brilliantly. I would also like to address for you the balance of those images. In watching the Tao, we know that life balances the good with the bad, the happy with the tragic, and the darkness within the light. Many faith systems and philosophies tend to treat negative aspects of life with a passing glance. It is *so* difficult to plug into that ultra positive persona that has been sold to us while sweeping the realities of our everyday existence under the rug. Taoism makes no such promises. It merely asks that you look at everything, accept it all, and learn from each side of the balance. In understanding this concept, there is wisdom in *all* we experience.

While it is easy for you to follow those happy thoughts and descriptions, you are processing in your life right now many dark and deep events that need some perspective. The question arises in your mind, "How does this tragedy I am experiencing fit into this?" You feel that you cannot entirely get into the message with this weight you are carrying. Let me paint some darker images, and portray a Taoist response to them, that balance is achieved here with a deeper understanding of the Tao, which you can apply to your daily events.

A damaged marriage -

My deepest sympathies go out to you here. From our humble beginnings, we have a natural desire to bond to another human being. Our most delicate memories are those of special connections, which we have built with special people in our lives. It is the most exquisite dance, the one of two energies, in unison, sharing common goals and destinations. But when the harmony is broken, the opposite effect occurs. Pure misery and sorrow replaces our once magical state. What can be done?

Let us first look at desire, both our partners and our own. As time moves forward, events, appearances, and needs change. New challenges present themselves. If we do not process these events in unison with our partners, the system begins to decay. Lack of communication becomes paramount in this event. Eventually, a separation becomes the only option, as too much damage has been done.

Our desires have a significant role here. First, analyze your own desires. Make a list—this will only take a few minutes. Write down all of the goals you wish to achieve, and how and when you want to achieve them. Be honest with yourself. You may find there are hidden things in your subconscious that are causing you to act out of character. Is there anything on your list that is primarily a self-gratifying goal? In understanding the Tao, we have learned that these desires often bring us unhappiness. They are a prerequisite and a condition for happiness. Are we too proud to tell ourselves "This is a selfish desire, and it is causing me unhappiness, I let it go, and paradoxically it frees me?" In assessing our partnerships, try to hold your own viewpoints with some suspicion. We can never be objective enough to accurately portray our own self-image.

Now list your partner's desires that you are aware of. How do the lists match? If both of you are willing to release some desires that are causing you both unhappiness, it becomes a win–win scenario. Most unhappiness in marriage is caused by one or both partners seeking satisfaction from outside themselves, with only their own self-interests in mind. Here the small self has been very busy. It is an insatiable character that demands from us selfish desires for its own needs. Listen to your heart carefully. If the small self is our master, then we truly have become the slave. Only with great wisdom and true humbleness in your soul can we be free of the small self, which whispers from deep within the backs of our minds.

In order for a consolation to begin, both parties must want it and be willing to work it out. Compromise, sacrifice and communication are the secrets to a successful marriage.

If this is no longer possible, then truly you have reached an impassible gorge, which cannot be crossed, and you suffer. A Taoist looks at all situations uniquely and makes no predetermined opinions. Each situation is unique and must be treated with the tools at hand. There is no one answer, no correct answer, and no wrong answer. We ultimately must decide for ourselves.

I have seen many unusual relationships. In these, people have witnessed them and questioned as to why they went on for so long, and what the purpose of it all was. When viewed from the outside observer, there was much disharmony involved. To that I can only respond this way. We all have the option and the ability to end a relationship at any time. We have the ultimate authority. If these two people choose to stay in this bond, then they *both* feel that they are getting something out of it that has enough value to where a separation is undesirable. It is not my place to judge here, and as a Taoist, I accept the choices that you have made for yourself.

All avenues must be pursued to determine that a termination is the only solution. For some relationships, termination is a very good thing. Both parties have taken some very hard lessons with them and having moved forward in their lives, they discover other sources of happiness that far exceed all they have ever known.

At this point, I would offer you this much to consider. Some events in our lives just happen, and are out of our control. In this case, we cannot control the actions of another human being. They have their own drummer that they must march to. If we can no longer stay in step with our companions, then they have chosen a different path. We may try desperately to try and salvage a broken relationship, but sometimes there is nothing more that can be done. Know when it is time to let it go. If you have lived an honorable life, lived selflessly, and continually try to improve yourself and are considerate to others, then take comfort in knowing that true happiness will come to you in another form. This time, it was simply not meant to be.

In time, a gift will be revealed for us to understand why this event has come into our lives. Take consolation in the fact that all is not revealed to us immediately, and we will in time see the "Big Picture" of this event. Assess the situation as you wave goodbye. Actions that you may have contributed in this parting, reconcile to yourself with the knowledge that you will not repeat them again, thus causing additional suffering in your life.

This is a difficult concept to convey, so try and understand patiently with me now. As humans, one of our biggest failings is seeking satisfaction and validation from outside of ourselves. We endlessly search for people, places, careers and love that can fill the void in our hearts that continually calls out "I am not adequate or complete." In dealing with our partners, assess accurately your needs and demands that you desire. For you to ultimately be happy, I present to you this one unequivocal truth.

Contentment and happiness can only be found from within yourself, nowhere else.

It is our destinations and lessons in life that help us uncover this truth, but the source is found deep within your heart. There is not a single element of happiness and contentment that you cannot find inside of yourself. It is all there, right where it has been from the moment you were born. As your self-discovery progresses, you will see this for yourself as the truth.

We seek validation from our partners in life. Perhaps unfairly, we expect them to fill the void in our heart that keeps calling out. When we grieve for this broken connection, we are silently acknowledging that our true inner self needs support and validation from outside of ourselves. That is very normal and understandable. I urge you to consider the fact that as we come to recognize this truth within ourselves, we can learn to release a broken relationship and you will feel less like losing a part of yourself with it. You are a complete and remarkable soul that has been given a set of unique challenges to overcome in your lifetime. The closing of a door on a relationship, though painful now, can open other doors in your future where you need to travel. We must learn to accept this in our understanding of the Tao.

If a relationship is truly over, then begin building that bridge to cross the gorge that lies in your path. On the other side of that gorge lies your future, and all of the infinite possibilities that are waiting patiently for you. You lie here in pain, a victim of the past. Find the strength to build that bridge. In time, your heartache and suffering will heal. Time is the great healer and is your best friend. With time, all can be overcome. There will forever be a scar. It is there to remind us of our past that the lessons in it will not be forgotten. We will have many more before this life is over. Do not let your present hold you from your future. It is always your choice to make. Conversely, we will also enjoy untold happiness in many countless hours that lay before us. All things happen in proper proportion, at the proper time. If we shift our focus to the future and all of the endless possibilities that could be our potential destinies that exist in a yet unformed state of flux, we allow a crack in the door for the universe to slip in and provide us with a future we can only dream about. The dream is the beginning. You travel the distance from idea to reality through understanding and perspective. With proper attitude and consolation, we begin our passage to better times.

Take comfort in knowing that you are on a low end of your learning cycle of life. In time, with proper understanding, you may take what you have learned and build yourself a stronger, happier, and more complete future. In the beauty of the Tao, all things are understood. How much we must endure to complete this life! I share with you now, a moment of silence, a silent prayer to the universe, that more positive energy will come your way. In the endless cycle of the Tao, it will surely happen.

The passing of a loved one –

We have been born into an existence that is limited in both time and knowledge. Our whole lives we seek out answers to questions, and solutions to our problems. In this fixed span we are given, there lies the opportunity for us to justify our own existence in the universe.

"Where do we go in the afterlife?"

"Why are we here?"

"What am I supposed to be doing with my life?" We all have these questions. There never seems to be enough time to do everything we want. We wish we had more time to spend with our dearest friends. Our questions remain unanswered.

When a member close to us in our whirlpool of life suddenly departs, an enormous void is left behind as the energy is transformed into the Tao. Several things happen now simultaneously. First and foremost, we selfishly miss this person, whose footprints will forever remain in our hearts. They can never be replaced. But how special their existence in our lives was while they were here! You cannot imagine that experience missing from your life. To honor that greatness, we must grieve. That is an expected and a completely natural emotion that has been given to us to process our lives. Again, we must remind ourselves that we are selfish in our loss. We miss the companionship and value that this person has brought into our lives. In time our sorrow will fade, but the memory will exist eternally. That also is acceptable. It honors all that they were in our lives.

Secondly, all those questions that have been drifting about in our minds resurface, and they begin to demand your attention. Death has a way of reminding us that we should be considering answers to these questions. There is a deeper meaning to our lives, and a tragic loss drives us to seek resolution, that we can justify and reconcile these events for ourselves.

When the body passes, and physical life no longer is maintained, the energy that is the soul, the person who you communicate with inside yourself every day, is passed on into the Tao. Remember your science class in high school. "Energy is neither created nor destroyed." And so it is. Their deliverance is all part of the natural process of life. In that moment of death, another life was born. All in the endless cycle of the Tao, the ten thousand things are born into fruition, and absorbed again. It has occurred since the beginning of time and will go on forever.

Our time on earth is fixed; we cannot extend it. It is that way for a reason. There is much for us to learn in this life. There is much to learn in the next. We tend to hang on to life in Western thinking with a tenacious grip that this existence is all that there is. I assure you, it is only the beginning. If we knew with certainty the next life was indeed so much more, so incredibly amazing, would it not loosen the grip that we so tightly hold on to in the present? We have a purpose here in this life that ultimately each one of us has to complete in their own way. When the work is done, our peace will surely come, for that is the form that all of nature has taken, and man is no exception. When the correct time has come we will cross over, it is that simple. We fear the unknown. We have no "scientific" proof, but we have many signs, and overwhelming evidence that there is more, so much more beyond.

Let your mind become as still as water.
See your heart in its depths.
Observe that in life there is death.
And within death there is life.
And all things follow their true paths,
Through the cycle known as the Tao.

Returning to the source is the way of nature.
In deception, you falter in confusion and sorrow.
In enlightenment you find in the depths,
A wisdom unseen,
A purity unknown,
A solitude unparalleled.

Now the dream becomes reality.

You are dignified as royalty,
Yet humble as a servant.
Impartial as the sun.
Benevolent as the moon.
You have found your own true self.

In the ocean of the Tao,
The current delivers all to their destinations,
And in death, we welcome our deliverance.

From Chapter 16 of the Tao Te Ching

The entire cycle of life is made up of various elements in constant motion. Change is our only constant. As we attempt to hold on to all of the "good" things in our lives while we collect more in the times that have become our existence, we find that there is a balance to how much we can grasp. The cycle known as the Tao relentlessly brings us what was meant for us, even if we do not recognize it or want it. As our loved ones slip back into this stream and flow once more to their own destinations, let us have the depth and understanding of the Tao to sustain us as we all complete our own journeys.

I take great comfort in knowing that my departed companions and I will meet one day again on the trail in the future. Let us honor their memories, that we were so fortunate to have had them in our lives. The Tao places all the correct events in our path that we require to progress as complete humans. May we recognize these events and celebrate our experiences. In our grief for our loved ones, let us not say "Goodbye," but "Until we meet again."

Illness and injury – Human suffering

Here I may speak from experience, with depth and understanding. In my youth I suffered from Spinal Meningitis and was paralyzed from the waist down for a year. In my forties I have suffered from Lymphoma in my chest cavity, and have undergone intense chemotherapy and radiation treatments. As a complication of radiation close to my heart, I have also suffered a heart attack. While still in the recovery process, my prognosis is good. My wife has suffered from Lupus for over thirteen years now, and has recently been diagnosed with Cerebral Vasculitus and also Ankylosing Spondylitis, another autoimmune disorder with long-term complications. Her destiny is always unclear. I am sure you have your own experiences that you can relate to here.

I have been both the patient and the long-term caregiver. In this time, I have observed many things and experienced the entire array of human emotions with suffering and all of the repercussions associated with them. In coming to terms with these elements first hand, I would like to pass on my own Taoist views here.

First, no pain or suffering is intentionally brought into your life as a punishment or to create disharmony in your existence as a result of offending some higher deity. Taoists believe in no judgmental or wrath giving power. There is a cycle that encompasses all of life, its creation, its flourishment, and its deliverance back into the system known as the Tao. Within these cycles, the entire range of possibilities exist, in perfect proportion and in endless motion. To provide perspective to our lives, there are placed many conditions of offsetting balances.

We know pleasure. It carries with it a favorable connotation. Much of our life is spent in search of supplying our minds and bodies with an endless amount of its drug like addiction. Conversely, we also know pain. In all cases we avoid it whenever possible. There is nothing wrong with either of these scenarios. They simply are. We accept that. We also value one because of the other. Here we see the lesson of the Tao that Lao Tzu has pointed out for us.

We know beauty only because we have seen ugliness.

We know good because we have known evil.

Perspective is much more than a simple word. (Again we see the power of simplicity.) In knowing and experiencing all that there is in this life, the "bad" things show us how valuable the "good" things really are. I use these terms to communicate with you in terms of traditional Western thinking. In understanding the Tao, we live our lives with no preference to either element. They are both exactly the same, just polar opposites in the equation of life. Each has the proper value in it. No more and no less. The cycle of existence brings with it equal amounts of each into our lives. Too much pleasure will lead us down some very disastrous paths. Too much pain will cause us to lose our willpower and our objectivity. One cannot be known without the other. To a Taoist there is value in each, thus there is no distinction between the two.

I have known many people in my life who have had a favorable existence, yet are very unhappy. Conversely, I also know many people (my wife included) who have had severe challenges that would bring many a great man to his knees, yet they have found a way through, and are very happy and well adjusted in their lives. So we see that neither condition is exclusive to happiness and well-being. Life is about attitude. From now on, try thinking of events as neither "good things" nor "bad things." They merely are "things", with no positive or negative associations.

"That's sounds just great!" you say. "Then *you* take this misery for awhile!"

If it was in my range of possibilities, I would gladly take all of the pain from the world, but that would lead to an imbalance in the Tao. So what do we do about it?

Make the most of your situations and learn from the lessons that are hidden in these experiences. Learn to endure. If you are enjoying a healthy life, by all means, appreciate it! If not, look deeper and draw out all of the lessons you have learned. Adversity has some interesting affects on humans. The most intense and captivating people I have ever met all suffered deeply at some point in their education of life. But by applying themselves, they have found a way to overcome the pain and look past the hardship to gain insight to answer their questions of life and what to do with it. If we all lived lives in perfect health with no problems ever, what would we have learned from our existence? That is the beauty of understanding the Tao. We see our place and our purpose here in this reality.

In looking closely at every detail of our lives, our questions are ultimately answered by understanding the Tao. It leaves nothing for us to wrestle with. Most people often overlook a living philosophy. It doesn't seem too glamorous; it is much too simple to have value in their minds. Whatever faith system you decide is correct for you, consider all the possibilities objectively. If your questions remain unanswered, this is your conscience hinting to you that a more complete solution lies out there.

Adversity can be a rather cruel teacher. Though the hard lessons of life take us to our knees, and each lesson pounds our souls like a hammer, we have the ultimate choice to take this energy and forge the key to our futures that we will be stronger and wiser. Here we may make that key that will open that door that has been closed to us, the lesson of the crisis our gift—if we choose to accept it. When faced with the prospect of laying in sorrow before the door that has become our challenge, is there really any other choice to make?

We have an ultimate responsibility to ourselves, to be the most happy and complete person we can be. In the light of our happiness and in the shadows of our darkest moments, let our spiritual teachers explain all that we want desperately to understand in this life.

In My Silence

I am a man, not a God
I am weak, but it has forever endured

I know so little
But need so much.

I know I am an image of some greater thing
If only I could know
what it is I am supposed to do.
In my weakness, I feel a strength
that whispers softly,

"You can be so much more."

JR

In explaining the balance of life that is pain and suffering, it is often misunderstood that we are trivializing our fellow mans unfortunate condition. I am not trying to belittle the pain in your lives here, trust me. I am trying to give you perspective that will allow you to use these events to make yourself stronger. In learning the lessons from Lao Tzu, there is the common thread that all things have value. To overlook this value is to have suffered for no reason. As long as we must have pain, let us also have virtue and understanding to sustain us.

"The only way to pass any test is to take the test. It is inevitable."

Elder Regal Black Swan
- From the wonderful book Mutant Message by Marlo Morgan

Life is very much, the most difficult test that we may ever take. We are constantly challenged to understand it and simultaneously be content and happy despite all of its most difficult paths that we have been challenged to travel. The greatest tool I can give to you in taking this test is one of perspective. If we keep one eye on the "Big Picture" of the universe as it appears on the morning horizon, then we have the comfort of understanding to sustain us in knowing that life is a balance. When the sun sets, we will not have missed the encompassing blanket of beauty that passed over us while we were busy focusing on our own trivial interests.

In our development as humans, we reach a point in our lives where we stop and say to ourselves, "There is something missing from my life!" You feel incomplete, unhappy and disillusioned with the way things have gone for you, and you want so much more out of life than you know how to get.

A Taoist watches quietly from his solitude, and smiles in gentle understanding. In releasing all of his desires, in understanding that the darkness of the night is followed by a brilliant sunrise, he endures all suffering with indifference. It is his perspective that allows him to look past whatever immediate sorrow that is lying in his path. It is only with compassion and perception that we may conquer all of our challenges. In understanding the balance of the good within the bad, he truly is never unbalanced in his life. These are not idle words. Many a great man has grasped their power and changed his reality. May you too see this truth for yourself and become one with them.

The wisdom of the Tao is an ocean of understanding. It has been waiting patiently for you since before your birth, before man walked the earth, and before time itself. You are so very close now. All of the events in your life have led you to this moment. Enter and transform.

Daily Chores

"So how do I apply these things to my daily life? I have so many tasks to do during the day; I have no time for all this philosophy stuff!" I am smiling right now while I am writing this, because I fully understand your situation. We have such complicated busy lives now, that we literally become lost and sometimes enslaved to them.

I urge you first to simplify. Cut back on the number of non-value added events you have taken on. The overuse of our personal hobbies has distracted us from our true paths. You could spend more time at home where you are needed and you can still balance your outside interests; it is time to reprioritize. Figure out what things you do that only fill your own desires, and cut these back. Apply this time saved to helping other people instead of serving yourself. That includes your family, for they need you the most. Give yourself to them. Literally, it is the greatest gift you have to give. That means spending time with them, being an active participant in their daily schedules, and *listening*. Listening is a lost art. I believe partly because we have become too caught up in ourselves.

A Taoist is an excellent listener. She has no interests of her own. She is focused on the people in her daily life, not on herself. Our own selfish interests outweigh our spouse's daily chatter, and we tune out. Give yourself to them—it is the lesson of the Tao in perfect execution. You will not be disappointed in the results.

In our lives, we have many daily tasks to perform. Most are not very glamorous. Washing clothes, doing the dishes, sweeping the floor, our first approach is to treat these with disdain. But in understanding the Tao and allowing it to come through us into our actions, our daily chores become fun also! By taking pride in a job well done, no matter how trivial, we are receiving from ourselves a positive attitude, one that in turn shines on every part of our daily existence. When your day is done you can look back and feel great about how much you have accomplished and know that you have made a difference, if only to yourself. Your positive attitude is your own immediate reward, but as we have learned, our actions come back to us full circle, and we will receive benefits later as well.

We must not become workaholics, but we also must be vigilant and not become lazy. Again, we must achieve balance in order to be happy. This is true not just in our psychological approach to life, but also in our daily chores. Our daily activities and our approach to them should mirror our inner spirit. If I search for happiness through dedication and vigilance in my mind and thoughts, then so too should I reflect it in my work. Both the mind and the body must work in coordination for us to reach a steady state of contentment. If I hold a task with disdain, then it will reflect this into my attitude as well. My thoughts and attitude are too valuable to me to be given away to a mere task that must be performed. I will not let it steal my happiness, thus I give myself to it that I may continue to control my own destiny. It is merely perspective, but we find that perspective is the cornerstone of discovery and true happiness.

It really comes down to dedication. In today's society, we seem to have lost many values that past generations used to measure themselves. Integrity, honor, devotion and loyalty; where have they gone? I feel a little like the last cowboy riding off into the sunset, knowing his time has gone. The world has changed, but I firmly believe these values never go "out of style." They are endangered, but certainly not extinct. I encourage you to evaluate your own life style. Do you honor these morals like you can? By taking pride in each task we do we are acknowledging our own hard work that we perform every day. Since we serve the world, we perform even the most mundane tasks with the knowledge that we are performing a selfless service. When sleep comes at the end of the day, we close our eyes and welcome it peacefully with open arms and sleep the sleep of an honest man. There isn't a cowboy left who wouldn't agree with that.

Truthful words are not attractive.
Attractive words are not truthful.
A good man holds his own opinion with suspicion.
Suspicious men hold fast to their own ideas.

The sage places no value on his possessions.
The more he does for others,
The more others do for him,
And his happiness is overflowing.
The more he gives away,
A value greater than wealth is returned.

The Tao brings all things to men,
Yet makes no claim.
The sage leads men back to the Tao.
A servant of the servant,
And leads from behind.

Chapter 81 of the Tao Te Ching

Now that we have a window into the Taoist view, I would like to show you a very simple application of how this works in her everyday world and perhaps yours too. The Taoist knows that she is a servant to the world. By sending all of her resources out into the world, and expecting nothing in return, her desires and requirements for happiness have vanished! With no expectations and demands that the universe must provide each day to keep her in good spirits, she becomes a very happy individual by the mere act of her giving. Paradoxically, the more she gives away, the more life provides for her! But how can this be? It is time now for another story from my collection.

I received a very sad phone call from a close friend one day. His mother-in-law had just succumbed to cancer, and he and his wife were understandably heartbroken. Words can never take that kind of pain away, but I tried my best to console him.

When I hung up the phone, I felt very empty and dark. I had perhaps taken just a small amount of their sorrow and it filled me deeply with compassion to want to heal them in some form. Using the craft of placing words ever so delicately into a very deep and moving verse, I reached inside my soul and pulled out a piece of myself and framed it into words, that we may share the burden together and let them both know how deeply I cared for them and their loss. I felt very relieved when I had finished this verse, because in some way it had changed my sorrow into a positive action. In this action I could perhaps make a small difference in their lives. I felt it was all that I could do, and hoped it would make a difference in their grieving. I then mailed the poem along with a short message the next day.

The day arrived for the memorial service. I walked in and began examining all of the many pictures of God's new angel. She had left behind quite a legacy of love, and I was deeply moved by the stories of a woman that had parted this life leaving such a void in these people's lives.

As the service progressed, the speaker made a special announcement during the eulogy. A poem that had greatly affected my friends was selected to be read; one that they claimed consoled them beyond words. It was indeed my poem.

I was surprised, humbled, and just a little shocked as the audience reacted to the speaker's very personal reading of those words I had struggled to carve from my soul. The climate in the room was absolutely breathtaking. The faces around me had transformed into a very calm and deeply compassionate tone. The gift from my heart had suddenly leapt off those pages and changed these peoples mood. Though a momentary comfort, I had made a difference in a very large and unplanned way.

After the service, many strangers approached me and wanted to personally thank me for my contribution. I was speechless. When I met my friends in the final reception line, I felt their sorrow, and knew that I had made a difference. With a warm kiss on my cheek, we exchanged wordless glances and in that moment touched each other's hearts forever. It was a very heart warming experience for me and one I will never forget.

Through one small act, I had affected dozens of people's lives. I had received a thousand fold return on but one small act selflessly performed. Lao Tzu's teaching had reaffirmed itself for me yet again in my life. The more we give away, the more we receive. If we pursue our happiness with a positive mind and an open heart, surely even the smallest tasks we perform have value and meaning. Let your work reflect the tranquility inside of yourself. Show the world your beauty in every task you have been given. It reflects to the world on the outside of you all the beauty that is found inside. In leading by example, we may create an Eden here on earth. The act of giving of yourself is but one more important stepping-stone in our walk of change.

Inside Yourself

So who is this voice that has played in your head? It has been there since your earliest memories. Surely you must know it by now. Or do you? Your mind represents your spiritual self, your soul. It is beyond description. In the whole universe, is there anything more mysterious and fascinating? Your soul is pure energy. It is untainted and unstained. No sin casts a shadow upon it. It is the core of all human existence. By definition, mind and soul are one. It inhabits your body with a distinctness that is called your personality. As we make choices in our life, our personality becomes more defined.

"But this is who I am!"

Are you so sure of this? Is it not really the collection of choices that reflect who you have become? That's right, I said choices. We all have the right to choose. We make hundreds of choices every day. Do you know that you choose your own level of happiness? It is a conscious decision we make to be happy. The level and consistency of happiness is totally up to you, it always has been.

"But I have all these things that make me unhappy!"

Or are they merely events beyond your control that you have chosen to be limits on yourself? If I let something bother me, surely it will. If I choose to accept it as something beyond my control, then I continue on in my contentment. Never worry about anything beyond your control. It will only distract you.

In the next section, we traverse a very integral and personal path within my garden. Within our minds lay the very keys we have searched our entire lives for. Through this path I would like to lead you to what you have sought after. The most difficult part of our journey is learning to recognize these keys when they present themselves.

Life is very much a puzzle, and we work the pieces we have been given one day at a time. When we become distracted by life and all of its crazy events, we become frustrated because nothing seems to fit together. Remember that not all the pieces are given to us at one time. Portions of our lives we wish to complete may not be here for us yet. We must use patience and understanding in these moments and work with what has been given to us. In time, our picture will complete itself. Sometimes we do not like the picture that is unfolding, and we desperately try and force our pieces into new arrangements. Here there are gaps, holes, and unfulfilled futures. Using these techniques, we can never see our true destinations and purpose.

There are several pieces I am giving you to use in your search, and it all begins with the most important one I have. It is intangible, invisible, silent and without form. It is contagious, self-fulfilling and the secret to every success that has ever existed. It is called positive attitude.

Positive Attitude

I had just finished college and was starting a new job. Needless to say, I was a young greenhorn who had much to learn. My new boss led me to a series of introductions with all the employees, and here I met an interesting man. He was the shop foreman and his name was Big John. While being large in stature, he also was very intimidating and rough looking. My hand disappeared as he shook it. They were the hugest hands I had ever seen. His appearance was very disheveled, but he had a unique manner about him and his gaze was riveting. After the boss walked away, it was just Big John and I.

"Let me tell ya a little secret son," he whispers. "I got a little piece of advice that you can take with you no matter where you go in life."

I stared at him curiously, not knowing what to expect next.

"Now I know ya don't know everything there is about what this job is gonna take, but neither do I; and I have been doing it for over thirty years! It's called fake it till ya make it!" he whispered. His eyes glanced around the shop, making sure just the two of us could hear this revelation. He smiled at me like he had just given me the map to the Holy Grail. I nodded my head politely, attempting to understand.

"You don't have to be the best, or know everything there is to get raises and promotions in life. *You* don't even have to believe it!" John whispered. "You just gotta make *them* believe it!" as he points over to my boss and the owners who were eyeing us curiously. At that he let out a huge chuckle that shook the walls.

"No matter what happens, you divert the blame so it never looks like you caused any problems" he continued. "Before long, they will think you are valuable and a real keeper. You can name your raises, and rule this place!" At this he let out a huge roar! It really startled me, and I began to understand a little of how the business world was going to be.

"Man, they never teach you this stuff in school!" I remember thinking. Looking back on that day, there was some truth and value to part of what Big John was saying. Now keep that thought as I tell you another story that will bring this together.

Many years had passed by, and I was at another job. My coworkers and I had been together for many years, and new employees were very rare. But in one day walks this young lady, smiling and shaking hands with about fifty male skilled trades' veterans in an hourly United Auto Workers garage. Talk about throwing the sheep to the wolves!

"This is going to be good," I remember thinking. Sure enough, things started happening. They really gave this girl a hard time. For weeks they had used their arsenal of practical jokes and sometimes cruel tricks on her. It was their way of letting her know that women were not wanted here and never could compete with men in this job. It actually shocked me at times. Guys that I had great respect for were showing this really ugly side of themselves. I actually think they might have felt threatened. My boss finally gave this apprentice to me for a while.

"If you say she can make it, I'll keep her," he whispered to me, and so it began. Mary and I began working that day. I began to notice as the weeks passed, that nothing ever seemed to bother her, and the crew had really turned up the heat. Now being associated with me did offer some relief and protection (which is why my boss assigned her to me) but they were relentless nonetheless. Finally I noticed a crack in the armor one day after a pretty embarrassing "joke" upset her. She went outside for a while and came back as if nothing had happened, smiling and talking to those that would let her.

"How do you do it?" I finally asked her. "Anyone else would have walked away months ago." With this incredible smile, she looked at me before replying.

"You just gotta fake it till ya make it!" I was literally stunned at this! My mind flashed back ten years ago to my first day on the job. Could she have known Big John?

"Even when they get to me, I don't let it show, because I'm not going to give them the satisfaction of knowing they hurt me," she continued. "On days when I'm really happy, it's really me you see. On days when I am down, I show you the same person, because faking my happiness eventually cheers me up and I return to normal at some point in the day. It's how I control it all. Eventually it is a genuine happiness more and more and I seldom have to fake it. You will become what you project." I still remember her smile staring back at me. I must have looked like I had just seen a UFO.

First Big John, and now Mary; I had found two totally different people with some very unique ideas about how to be successful. I must admit I was skeptical at first. But at this time in my life I was really searching for ways to effect change in my attitude. By being positive, or at least projecting it at first, could I possibly make it a permanent part of who I was? It did not seem very feasible, but I began my experiment.

Mary had been right about several things. First, it was hard to get it started. I needed her "model" of positive thinking to reinforce my early attempts at this approach. But in time, I really began to be more positive, just by pushing myself and struggling with that old negative demon that liked to take over every day. I cannot tell you how effective this really became for me. It was the beginning of my search for answers to all the questions I had been asking to no one in particular my whole life. My coworkers noticed. My friends noticed. My family noticed. Some days I could not pull it off so well, but I kept trying. Slowly I got better and better at it. My mood actually began to permanently change to being positive! It was a very gradual change, yet in time it did come. These things can be difficult to measure. It is like sunlight streaming in through a window. Gradually, ever so slowly it creeps across the room until morning is in full bloom. You never are quite sure when it came about, but you will know when it happens.

With a new attitude, new doors began opening for me. These were doors I had never seen or known before. It was the beginning of my self-exploration that has changed me forever. But is it really change? Is it not just uncovering who I really am? Think about that for a moment. Are we not just frustrated in life because we cannot entirely remove the shroud of society's dictations and beliefs and warped values from us so that our own real "true" self is uncovered? If you accept that there may be some truth to this statement, does it not drive you forward to find a deeper introspection, a journey you should set out upon to find your own true self?

Have you at times in your life had the feeling that there was something else going on that you just couldn't quite put your finger on? Could there be a bigger picture that you just weren't seeing? I can best describe it as a sound. A beautiful intricate rhythm beyond description that blows through my spirit and touches my very soul; it draws me from all the clamor of daily life. As long as I remain centered, continually I feel it surrounding me. When you learn to accept the lessons of the Tao, everything makes *so* much sense, and that gentle note that you used to hear on occasion, becomes a melody that plays in your heart every moment, every breath, and every step you take. It is an indescribable rich symphony of every wavelength that the universe sends out, coming through in the most intricate and captivating patterns. You live your life now tuned to listen to this music, that it will forever be yours to hold. It literally is a world within your world. Most live and die without ever finding it.

"If a man does not keep pace with his companions, perhaps it is because he hears a different drummer. Let him step to the music which he hears, however measured or far away."

Henry David Thoreau

Oh how I want to take you all there! I can only leave you this book as a map, a direction for those that seek it out. Ultimately, we all must conquer the mountain on our own. There is nothing more fundamental in this quest than beginning with a positive attitude.

In our search for who we really are, we struggle with many issues and questions from our past. As you are learning in this text, life is a balance. All of our experiences have lessons and gifts for us to accept. Please come to terms with these past issues that you may free yourself to explore the future. You can do nothing about your past, but yet you can control everything about your future. Spend your energy where it is most effective. You will need all of your resources to fully engage the quest for change. There is more to you than you think. Your old self-image is about to make a miraculous transformation. Much like a caterpillar spinning its cocoon, it prepares by gathering its strength and leaving its past behind. In time, with much hard work and persistence, the butterfly will emerge. An artist, a musician, sculptor or dancer may lie within. If you have always wished more for yourself, then what is holding you back? I will tell you a secret to how I have been successful.

"How did you learn to do that?" people ask me.

"Easy, I never listened to anyone who told me that I couldn't!" I replied. In my mind, I have always had the ability to be a musician, an artist, a poet and a writer. I just had to sit down and apply myself without letting setbacks get me down. It takes time to learn new skills, but patience, positive attitude, and a will to succeed will make the difference.

Even if you are not the best at what you apply yourself to, it makes no matter whatsoever. As long as it makes you happy, then by all means, carry on! I have never believed in limitations on myself. By believing all things are possible, you open a door to the universe that everything may enter!

Positive energy attracts positive energy. It is like a magnet once you turn it on. People around you will engage you in conversation just to get that energy you are projecting. Perfect strangers will reach out, curious enough to expand from behind their quiet withdrawn shells. A positive attitude is like a wind that grows into a hurricane, taking everything it touches with it. It all starts with the breath that is little old you. Amazing, isn't it? The more positive you become, the more energy you have, and the more fun life will become!

"But I'm not really like that."

"I'm too quiet and it's not my personality to be that outgoing."

"People are just too hard, I don't like rejection, and so I just walk while looking away."

"But I am in poor health, and suffering is just too hard. I have the right to be miserable!"

All of these comments I have heard and understand. I know. I used to use them myself. I used to be so meek that I couldn't even use a telephone! I also began writing this book while undergoing chemotherapy and radiation treatment for cancer, quite the contrast from one extreme to the other. The power of positive energy is incredible. Once you understand the Tao, you will see how people function, and understand that your own pain has a place and a role in your development as a human.

Accepting negative energy cuts you off from all of the positive energy that the universe is sending your way. A new thought should have just presented itself to you in that last sentence! You *accept* negative energy. Only you can allow sadness to enter your heart. It is a choice we make as to whether we accept it or not. You have the ability to say to the world, your friend or just yourself, "I thank you for your gift of negative energy, but I refuse to accept it." At this point it disappears, a phantom into the shadows. Your day continues on in its solitude. While this may seem overly simple, do not underestimate the power hidden within the concept. Our perceptions change our realities.

It is time now for another story. My great friend J.J. and I used to walk every day during our work break for exercise. We would walk perhaps twenty-five minutes while we discussed the current issues of the day. Observations of the weather and the seasonal changes were the basis of our talks. But something unique began to transform during our time together. As the years went by, we discovered that the walks had become much more than just keeping our bodies in shape. We used that time to express ourselves, and had become very familiar with who lived in each other's hearts. I had discovered that this man was one of the purest souls I had yet in this life to meet. We enjoyed each others company, and it was with each day that we would walk rain or shine, side by side.

While we were very comfortable with each other, it was very natural to talk about things that were bothering us in our daily jobs. While this can be very beneficial in our life to have this outlet, we both had become aware that it was detracting from our valuable time together, and placed a shadow on our once refreshing daily jaunts.

New rules for discussion were immediately formed once we realized this fact. No longer was work ever to be a topic. This changed our entire attitudes! Next, whenever one of us would start complaining about a personal event, we would stop the discussion and alert the other that this problem was ruining our day and our walk. It was OK to share a problem, but the other party would immediately apply perspective to it.

I would say, "J.J. you are letting this problem steal your day away from you. Don't let it run off with your happiness." It was like a wind clearing the clouds away, and the sunshine would come blazing back into our hearts.

"Thank you very much for that!" he would say as his attitude shifted back into high gear. While we think ourselves capable of monitoring our own attitudes, it just cannot be done. We cannot ever be that objective. J.J. and I returned from our walks always happier than when we left. Though our paths in life have since denied me this pleasure, I remember the lesson very well. It is one I shall remember forever in my heart.

You can justify anger or sadness easily. We feel that we are entitled to it. That is what we have been taught in this life, is it not? If something that is unpleasant happens to me, it's OK to be mad, isn't it? Let's study this concept for a moment. Here is an example.

I came home one day to find my daughter's car had broken down. While repairing it, I continued to find more items that needed attention, and the bill kept going up. To complicate things, I had injured myself while being frustrated with the slow progress. I was now running out of time and would miss my daughter's visit. After completing all of the repairs and totaling up the costs in my mind, I was not in a very good state of mind upon entering the house. My mood was bad, and my daughter's visit that I always value so much, was spoiled. She left feeling guilty because after all, it was *her* car that had caused it. My emotions had caused a block that I just couldn't let go, even if that meant upsetting her, which I certainly never intended to happen. I was right in being upset, wasn't I? Who wouldn't get mad, it was understandable, wasn't it?

The lesson here is that you can never accept negative behavior, even if you feel you are entitled to it. By blocking out the positive, you effectively cut off your happiness. Keep this in mind during your next tirade. Turn down the one gift and accept the other.

In your search for a more consistent attitude, I urge you to consider these observations. The less negative energy you expose yourself to, the easier it is to maintain your own balance. While this may seem obvious, we tend to frequently overlook this as a tool for self-improvement. Our culture continually bombards our senses with negative energy. If we can reduce our exposure to these energy-depleting sources, and replace them instead with positive things, we have taken that first step toward changing our perceptions and ultimately our own reality. In my search for a more consistent and controlled attitude, I have found a few helpful ideas for you to consider. While obvious in description, do not overlook their effectiveness in changing your life.

First turn off the nightly news, forever. The repeated daily reports of every murder, rape, abduction, and despicable human behavior have been well documented. What purpose does it serve in my life to be continually bombarded with their repetitive examples that I have no control over? Like a seasoned homicide detective, we have become immune and conditioned to accept the darkness of human behavior as just another highlight for the evening news. I hope my soul never stops being compassionate for my fellow man. Though I know these events will all cross our paths in our lives, we were never intended to be overrun with the endless tragedy of the world in these pre-administered doses. It draws your positive energy away from you, and inflicts you with its poisonous and contagious attitude. I am compassionate to all human suffering. As a Taoist, I help out whenever and whoever I can. I cannot save the world from itself. The most effective servant I can be begins with being mentally as strong and positive as I can. Use your energy where it is most effective. Push the power button to off.

This also applies to your daily newspaper. I have not read a paper for news content in over ten years. I feel I have not missed a thing. Conversely, I have enjoyed my improved attitude so much, that I have used that time quite well in changing other people's lives. Again we see the balance of the Tao here. While there are occasionally stories of value, I find myself pulled into reading the daily destructive behavior of my fellow man. It is my compassionate nature to continue thinking of these tragedies, long after they have occurred. I pray for their souls. I send my energy in their direction that the families will recover, that the children will forget and sleep a child's dream again someday. I pray that the policeman who had to respond to the scene can find the courage to return to work the next day, and stop the nightmares that plague him. I can quote you line by line some stories I have read, over twenty years ago. They have left a shadow on my soul. Tragic events I have read, that still bring tears to my eyes as I write this. In searching for a happier life, I have left this medium to itself. I choose not to share in the destructive force it brings to my well-being. I try to keep it to the comics, sports, the crosswords and maybe a movie guide. Everything has purpose; it is up to us to use it in an effective manner that can make our lives more positive.

> "And I am sure that I never read any memorable news in a newspaper. If you are acquainted with the principle, what do you care for a myriad of instances and applications?"

> *Henry David Thoreau*

The same goes for people with negative energy. You know who they are. You don't dare ask them how things are going. You will receive a fifteen-minute dissertation on how terrible their lives are. While an experienced Taoist may engage these people with minimal effect, it is not the place for those of us just finding our way to a more positive life. Meet them with a smile, a handshake, a warm greeting, and move along with your day. Engaging them will only draw your life force from you while you are pulled into their negative reality. Choose not to go there with them. In time, when you are much stronger, you may go back and attempt to plant some positive energy in them, that one day they can effect their own change. For now though, keep your visits short, all things in moderation. By limiting our exposure to negative energy from sources that are easily controlled, we have begun to shape our new attitudes in a more positive way. It is our own mental strength we are working on building here. Your priority should be your own well-being. We must first be strong before we can help others. A more positive attitude is just a cancelled subscription, the push of a button, and a quick wave of the hand away.

Let's talk about behavior a little more now. Most people's roughness is just a defense, an armor that keeps the world from penetrating too deep. They think it will keep the "bad stuff" away. They have become a prisoner in their own isolation. They live in a castle formed of blocks of stone that have become their defense mechanisms; rudeness a cornerstone, deceit the iron gate, impersonalization the mote of defense. There is no champion to save them. No hero can penetrate their defenses. When you meet a Taoist for the first time, the difference to your own life can be striking. They have removed all of the stones that would trap them within themselves. There are no defenses, that all may approach them. The power of complete understanding has brought them a calm and carefree yet responsible behavior. While they appear plain and unadorned, with no flags flying or banners claiming their greatness, they carry their beauty on the inside. With no expectations, they have no disappointments. This is the beauty and the power known as the Tao. There is nothing more that they desire. They have it all.

A Taoist returns to the purest form of herself; the child she once was. As a child, we trusted the whole world. Our needs were very simple. Our requirements for happiness were very small indeed. Every day was another chance to explore. Every object, no matter how simple, needed to be investigated and played with. In this stage of life, we have it all but do not know it yet. We mature, see man and society for what they are, and leave that smiling child behind, a forgotten memory. Though our experiences in life teach us many lessons we need to develop and grow, it is important to use the past and *all* of our memories to develop richer perspectives of who we really are. In the need to become happier in our lives, let us not forget that remarkable miracle of life we once were. Sometimes in our development, it is not who we have become and want to be in this life, but more of who we once have already been.

When I look into the eyes of this sweet child, I pray one day when she is struggling with her life that she may see this picture and understand the perspective of her experiences. The values and pureness of who we are is never lost, just merely covered in layers of our development. We just need to use the tool of introspection to remember who really lives inside of us. That child still lives within you. What a comforting thought for us to use in discovering our new positive attitude. Lets us hold it close as we would this adorable child. Each moment in our lives can be this rich!

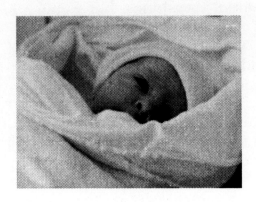

In learning the lessons of Taoism, your life will change. I guarantee it. You will become a traveler with no armor, no weapons and an extended hand. Being open like this is a little scary at first. Yes, you will get a rough reception in the beginning. But your openness leaves no place for their blade to enter. When they realize you mean only good and want nothing from them except a warm conversation, they begin to loosen up and put their weapons down. This may take time, so be patient. Keep chipping away every day. I have found very few people I could not win over with my sincerity.

The old "Golden Rule" still applies. Treat others how you want to be treated. It gets no simpler than that. The reflection of who you are is generally what is projected back to you. If you want better things to come your way, then send better things out into the world. You must give if you want to get. By consciously improving your attitude, you are effectively taking control of your world and reshaping it. It all begins with positive attitude. I would like to expand on an old idea that is very valid and deserves a revisit at this point in our discussion.

Perception is reality

How many times have we heard this? I want you to really focus on the depth of these three simple words. (Again we see the power of simplicity.) In our focus on positive attitude, we have found that whatever we imagine to be in our minds does indeed become our world. If I proceed daily with the thought that my life is depressing and has no possible good future, does that not in effect become my existence? The power of positive thinking and the energy it carries cannot be overstated. It is the seed from which all of your future will grow.

If I tell myself that things will work out for the best and that I will accept all that I cannot change, and that eventually all of life's purpose and events will be revealed to me, do I ever have any reason to be depressed? In effect, this way of thinking becomes your reality. The pessimists in life continually will argue their opinions though.

"You are only fooling yourself, these evils and bad things really exist and you are choosing to ignore them!" But I always counter.

"Then who is the wiser, the man who smells the roses and raises them for his family to enjoy, or the man who curses their thorns, and spends no time learning how to cultivate them?" Are the two realities not the same? Is it not our approach to life that dictates our happiness? So who is the wiser, the man that "knows" the realities of the hard work and the negative aspects, or the man who accepts the burden and makes it a beauty in his eye? Perception is reality. How we view events in our lives will dictate our own level of happiness. Look for the positive in all that comes our way. It is the power of our correct thoughts and deeds that will show us the true destinations meant for us in our journeys. Turn your attention to the positive energy in life. It is by far the strongest, and will take you the farthest.

Many books and methods have been written on this topic, and their points like mine are well taken and make sense, but what is lacking is a way to effectively implement them. The difference in my approach is the basic principles that are found in the Tao. We learn that all forces in life are to be respected and honored. We also learn that our own concerns and needs come last in our lives. In understanding and accepting these concepts, we must actively use them every day in order to honor their place in our hearts. In accepting that the universe has many hidden benefits and mysteries that will slowly be revealed to us, we come to a new understanding.

Life is not just about pain or suffering. It is not about self-indulgence and self-gratifying life styles and habits. It is not about gathering possessions that soon come to own us. The more importance you place on these things, the more power you give them over you. In understanding that life is a balance and that we must make the best with whatever it brings our way, we begin to accept a synchronicity that has permeated our lives. The correct thing will happen at the right time. It always does. That is the lesson of the Tao. With no struggles, we are just gently paddling our way down the stream of life. The river will take us to where we are supposed to be. Just let it happen. With this new understanding, a positive attitude is the *result* of tuning our thoughts into the Tao. It is both things in our journey, the basis of our beginning and the ultimate goal of our destination.

Happiness and positive attitude walk hand in hand. One will follow the other. If we seek to hold the elusive hand of happiness more and more, then we must bring our positive attitude to lure it. There can be no other more important destination in our lives. Though the sands of time have slipped past us, it is never too late. This very day, you may begin to change your world. With a positive attitude, we may find the beauty that mirrors the image of our own souls. The synchronicity we discover is our hearts aligning ourselves to the world around us. Here we may not only see, but feel the pureness and power of positive energy. The choice is ours.

Our tendency in the West is to spend our time worrying about tomorrow. Though tomorrow arrives, its mysteries never match our expectations. While it is important to plan somewhat for the future, we must not let the daily revelations of each act as it is played out before us, draw our attitudes away from us. Let us learn to enjoy *today's* sunrise with whatever it may bring. All of life's gifts meant for us will come! There is no need to be concerned for what we do *not* have. In looking over the horizon for our ship to arrive, we overlook the one that is waiting just before us! In 24 BC, the Roman poet Horace writes:

"Carpe diem, quam minimum credula postero."
"Seize the day, put no trust in tomorrow."

Horace

In concentrating on just today, instead of all of our worries that may or may not arrive, we focus our energy on what we *can* control. Our minds can create many ominous shadows for us to run from. It is human nature. By reaching inside of ourselves and turning on the light of Awareness, we may enjoy a positive life with no shadows to worry about. Here we clearly can see now that perception is reality.

Is a great outlook on life and a happy spirit in our hearts not what all of us want of our lives? It really is our main goal in life, is it not?

If you struggle with a positive attitude as most do, be patient in your progress to change. Personality tuning takes serious dedication and hard work. I can assure you one thing though, it will be the most rewarding thing you have ever done. By yourself, for yourself, for your family, friends, community, and your world, your attitude displays to them all, "This is who I am!"

Joseph Roggenbeck

A Day on the Lake

I have a place in my mind that I would like to take you to now. Picture the surface of a lake. Think of all the things we see on a lake—people fishing, kids swimming, geese foraging for food. Waves gently bounce a group of newborn ducklings as they follow their relentless game of follow the leader. The sun reflecting off of the water and the gentle sounds of waves falling on the shore, the picture is very familiar to our memories.

In the distance we see also many boats, in many shapes and styles, going many directions and in many speeds. Picture yourself in your own boat, on the surface of this lake, which you must maintain in a safe condition. This is your life. As we travel our journeys of existence in these vessels that sustain us from harm, we face many challenges.

Always we must follow the current naturally, if we are to enjoy a balanced and natural life. But in the learning curve of our lives, we have tried unsuccessfully at times to direct our "boats" in directions that are not meant for us. When we met great resistance, one of two things happened. We either recognized our own troubles that we caused for ourselves and regrettably corrected them, or we continued on in our folly, only to cause ourselves more suffering and discontentment. The Tao is a river flowing naturally to us at all times. Recognizing the current and working with it instead of against it is the secret to living a balanced and content life.

It is hard to know when we are to paddle quickly, slowly or in what direction. The lake brings us some very large waves sometimes, and we are tossed about in wild abandon. Here we find that in these times, we must not panic, and must take proper action. Knowing first to point your boat into the wind and to paddle hard to safety is a learned behavior.

"When I have done all that I can, and the small self is quiet, then I am following the correct path."

In our early experiences in life, we leave the safety of the small inlets of our youth to venture farther and farther out into the depths of life's tides. After taking on a little water, and surviving a few close calls, we learn some lessons in handling our little boat of life. We find that there are times we must move quickly to avoid danger, and times that we may relax and enjoy the natural flow of the current. A Taoist hones these skills to a fine science. She lets life take her where it leads, but in the journey when trouble arises, she uses all of her skills and energy when the situation calls for it. She does not panic, for panic will only cause her boat to rock and make her own situation even more difficult. Her self-confidence that all things have a cycle that will return, and the strength of understanding the currents of the Tao will once again show her that she has a proper perspective of the lake and all that it will bring. Though she cannot change what the current brings, she holds the proper attitude to keep herself safe and in control. It is her self-confidence that is her reward, the jewel that the Tao holds for her.

With incredible self-discipline, she remains in control. The other vessels she passes in her travels even on calm days pitch and roll in precarious ways, all the results of the owners own incorrect actions. They are causing their own unhappiness and continually cry out for help. The Taoist sees these things at all times. When she can help without harming herself, she takes action. If she can show a man a better way to handle his boat, then she gives herself to it, and completes her own task in helping others.

There are some fellow travelers that cannot be helped. They will take your vessel down with them in their destructive behavior. Know when to recognize these events, and leave them to themselves. It is a wise sage that knows when he can do no more. Not all can be taught. That too is the cycle of the Tao. In the great lake of life, there are masters at their craft, and there are also many novices. Recognize that when your boat is taking on too much water, it is time to return to your own destiny, and leave your fellow traveler to his. The lake of life is bringing the correct events to you both. In these times, the troubled traveler must learn on his own.

At the end of day, the Taoist pulls her vessel to shore for the evening, and looks out on the lake at all she has seen. She helped those she could, and served as an example for those she could not. In the greatest storm, or the calmest day, she travels in self-confidence that in knowing the cycles of the Tao and her place upon the lake, that there is nothing to fear. That is the lesson of detachment that the Tao would show us. If you want to live in complete confidence with no fear ever, you must first trust in the balance of the Tao.

Lao Tzu reminds us of our need to continually focus not on ourselves, but on the great current known as the Tao. In doing this, we actually become the caretakers of the world, by the mere act of letting it go! Our immediate reward is one of a solid and absolute confidence that there is nothing to concern ourselves about. All things are taking their destined course, and by being a living extension of the Tao, we are one with it and enjoy the complete satisfaction that we are focused and in proper perspective.

Time will reduce your fear, as faith and understanding will guide your boat in complete self-confidence. Only through faith may we paddle through the river of fear. Self-assurance will now be the paddle you will use in guiding your own destiny. The lake is much calmer for you now! Let us enjoy it in our new-found perspective. In understanding all of this, we now can experience a relaxed and simple life that is easily balanced. Once we learn not to rock our own boats, things are so much simpler. That is the great secret of the Taoist.

In Mark 4:35, the story of Jesus on the lake is told. Here he is sleeping in the boat during a severe storm when his disciples cried out in terror.

"Teacher, don't you care that we are about to die?" Jesus stood up and commanded the wind.

"Be quiet!" and he said to the waves, "Be still!" The wind died down, and there was a great calm. Then Jesus said to his disciples, "Why are you frightened? Do you still have no faith?"

Even with Jesus by their side, the disciples allowed fear to control them. How can we expect to do much better? Learn to travel with confidence in life. We mistakenly have been led to believe that we need so many things to be complete in our search for happiness. In trusting that we really need only perspective to understand all that is around us, and acting properly to it will bring us complete control, we have gained an amazing confidence in our travels. Adversity has many lessons tc teach us. Though painful, there are times when we must accept that we must take a challenge on alone. This will build our own confidence in time, as we find out that our faith is rewarded by our emergence through our challenges. If a helping hand is always extended, we tend to use it, and we lessen the lesson. Be aware of this when it presents itself to you.

In my youth, there was a lake nearby that was very popular. Many ski boats would be zipping by, often driving very recklessly. There was a small inlet, where an old man could be found in his small boat with a fishing line in the water, and a large straw hat on his head. He would wave as we went by, and never complained as we rocked his boat with our errant waves.

One day, a boat had come very close to him, speeding recklessly while not paying attention to where they were going. Wham! We watched as the speeding boat bounced and slowly came to a halt. Then suddenly it began to sink! It had hit a pile of rocks that were just below the surface. As we prepared to launch a rescue mission, we watched as the old man maneuvered his boat carefully and pulled up to the floundering survivors. A ladder went over, and he pulled them all in. All matter of factly, and with an almost choreographed manner, the crew was rescued and taken to shore. As my cousin and I later met up with the old man, we found him quietly baiting his hook, and casting his line. He was so natural and composed; it left a very vivid memory in my young and impressionistic mind. As we tried to engage him in conversation, he just smiled, and checked his line. Finally, after realizing these two young chatter boxes were not going away any time soon, he set his pole down, and motioned us to come aboard.

"You see that little ripple, as the waves pass by over there?" he says. After looking at where he had been pointing, it suddenly became obvious.

"Oh yeah, I see it now!" I shouted. Just under the surface was a huge pile of boulders. Right next to it was a sign that read, "Danger! Hidden rocks below!" The old man laughed as he continued.

"Young folks today just aren't as smart as they used to be. I have been on this lake for over sixty years. Seems I pull more people off them rocks all the time. I know these people must know how to read, but they are just too busy running about, thinkin about themselves instead of paying attention to what's goin' on around them. They just don't look where they are going!" We nodded silently as he went on. "I usually wait for them to get a little wet before I pull em' out" he says. "Water puts a little fear in em' that God couldn't!" At this he laughed gently. "Hopefully you boys learned something here today."

"Yes sir!" we replied. That indeed was the truth.

In our day on the lake here in this text, there are similarities to that day of my youth. When we run about, so focused on our own little worlds, we forget to look at the "Big Picture" going on around us. Nature never forgets. We live by its laws, and she is the judge, the jury and the ultimate authority. As great a race as we imagine ourselves to be, we are at its mercy for our continued existence. One misplaced meteor could be the last chapter of the Earth. Our lives are startling vulnerable. Do not take for granted a continued existence of health and safety, nor the certainty that today will lead to another. A true traveler of life has prepared himself for all of these unforeseen events. Nothing surprises him. He merely reacts to them with the resources he has, with no predetermined ideas of what life is supposed to be. We live in an incredibly delicate world. We take for granted all of these blessings as a given right. Though it may be all you have known, it is not all that you may know. Being prepared for adversity while not putting ourselves in harms way, is the way of the Tao. Again we see the power of Wu Wei. Though we appear to be living our lives effortlessly, it is a result of correct action and behavior.

We have learned that only by proper action, a balanced behavior, and a simplistic lifestyle, may we navigate the lake that is our lives. Here we learn not only to survive, but also to thrive, in the face of all adversity. That is the great secret of the sage.

I hope to have given you a unique perspective with this little picture I have painted for you here. Proper perspective of life and all that surrounds us is one of the most difficult to convey. It is even harder still to own in our attitudes and perspectives. I wish you safe passage now. With calmer waters, a rich and satisfying journey lays before you.

A Night on the Shore

After our day at the lake, I would like to spend with you now, a quiet evening on the shore. This is all part of learning how to live a balanced life. We must take time to settle our minds and take in the stars that wait patiently every evening for us to ponder.

Though our small self always cries out for companionship, there is much to learn in traveling alone at times in our lives. There are times when I enjoy being alone, that I may watch the world quietly turn, and see myself sitting in its forest from above the clouds. It gives me perspective to allow for these moments of detachment. I enjoy my aloneness from my fellow man as much as I enjoy his companionship. All things in moderation bring us a balanced life.

Solitude is an amazing sage. It has relentless calmness. It allows us to tune out the waves of life and let our own vessel seek its own calm waters once again. Here we may once again find the gentle voices that are the subtle energies coming through. They are the whisper of the Tao, which wishes to guide us in the correct direction. Solitude is your tool back to discovering your true inner self. In knowing this, we may take the time to quietly watch the world for a few moments and reflect, instead of react. We react in a continual rhythm in our boats of life to the waves that constantly challenge us every day. Solitude places calm water under your ship in even the most raging storm. It gives you self-confidence that cannot be found in any other form.

Our lives today are so filled with activities and tasks that we never are allowed to really be by ourselves and just take the world in. This is where man has been led astray today. Solitude gives us a chance to turn off all of the noise and listen gently to the Tao and the subtle energies that continually try and push through all of the distractions that surround us. Give yourself to it regularly. It is the refreshment of the Gods. In listening to our own hearts beat in the quietest moments, we align our inner spirit again with our own true selves. Learn to enjoy these moments and seek them out for yourself. Solitude is the master of the great sage. Learn from its wisdom, it is an overflowing river of knowledge for you to enjoy.

"I never found the companion that was so companionable as solitude."

Henry David Thoreau

Some behaviors that have been given to us reflect a habit that we would do well to leave behind. The standard work ethic is relentlessly applied, and we are pressured to feel that we must constantly be doing *something*. A moment idle is a moment wasted. "So what did you do today?" is the common question. If we don't fill these moments up with tasks and trivialities, then somehow we have demonstrated some sort of failure or incompleteness.

The same goes for our plans and our futures. We seem to be on some sort of prearranged path that is well thought out and filled to the top with details that extend far out into our future. While we must plan for our futures, and keep our present in control, there is a clear and precise distinction between these realities and one of an over complex and sophisticated existence. We get so caught up in filling out these checklists, that when we do take a moment from our life to try and relax, we find that we cannot. Our minds race endlessly forward to all of the details of the moments we are losing that could be spent *doing* things.

To find our true selves and understand our purpose in life completely, we need first to communicate with ourselves. This begins by learning to sit still. It is that simple. Because the world travels at thousands of miles per hour, it doesn't mean that we have to. Yes there are times that this is necessary, but you must learn the balance to that is just taking time out from your life to just sit. With an open mind, go outside and pull up a chair. Watch the scenery for ten minutes. Listen to the birds call out to each other. See the clouds drift by in their endless journey. Smell the grass, the neighbor's campfire that lingers into the next day, the smell of fresh water upon the earth. Watch as the insects continue on in their own little world. Take on all the things you have been missing while you were checking off "to do" lists for the last ten years.

The measure of a man lies not only in all that he has done, but also in all that he has left undone. This is the rule of leading a balanced life. Our goal in life should be one of complete contentment. All else is folly. When we are dead and gone, who will remember the millions of trivial tasks we had completed in our overburdened life styles? Use your time wisely. In your life thus far, has accomplishing the entire myriad of trivialities and tasks you have been given (and taken on!) increased your happiness and well-being? Will continuing this pace bring you the happiness you desire? Given this observation, can you now understand the wisdom of Lao Tzu hidden in the message that he has left for us.

In pursuit of knowledge,
Man collects something every day.
In pursuit of the Tao,
The sage releases something every day.

He demands less of the world,
So the world demands less of him,
Thus balance is achieved,
And all things are as they should be.

The world has managed itself long before man.
Observe and watch the master.

Chapter 48 of the Tao Te Ching

What does it mean, "In pursuit of knowledge, man collects something every day. In pursuit of the Tao, the sage releases something every day." Taoists interpret this as man's continual need to interfere not only with nature, but also with all of the frantic demands that he has placed on himself. It seems our intrusive and controlling nature continually leads us down the difficult path. Solitude is one of the key ingredients we have left out in our search for the perfect recipe of life. Yes, life can bring you so much more. You just have to let it in! Take the time to understand the universe, and it will reward you far beyond a perfectly manicured house, or the image of success.

It is important that we recognize these events and the stirrings within us. Not every man feels this wind in his heart. But we must also react responsibly to them, as we seek perspective from this world. While searching for their spiritual answers, I have known many people who have completely reformatted their lives. If the answers they seek are not here, then they must lie somewhere else, and they disappear into the future. In interviewing these people later in life, I found some interesting admissions. It seems the overwhelming majority had picked up, moved to many exotic locations, engaged in many holistic and deeply involved spiritual practices and virtually changed everything about who they were in their lives. When I would ask them about the value of all of their efforts, to a man, they all agreed that all of the rewards that they had found for all their work could have been gained by remaining where they had been! I found this very intriguing. Some even admitted that it had delayed their progress in finding the answers that they had sought. Some had been on the right path the whole time.

Within the humbleness of your dwelling, the whole world can be known.
Without looking through the window, an entire universe can be seen.
Closing his mind, a man searches endlessly, for the Tao within his grasp.
For knowledge and understanding are two separate paths.

Thus the sage is wise in his stillness,

Holding eternity,
Seeing the unseen,
Knowing the unknown,
Achieving without appearing to do anything at all.

Chapter 47 of the Tao Te Ching

While an alternate future may hold the promise of immediate rewards, it is just not necessarily so. All we need to be complete as satisfied humans lies nearby. Do not search far for what is near. The Tao will always supply what we need, when we need it. We only need to keep an open mind and actively seek out solutions with moderation and understanding. Your solutions exist around you at this very moment. They are hidden at times, but they can also be very obvious and powerful. Look at events that come into your life with the understanding that there are no "coincidences." We may not understand the message, or recognize the messenger, but rest assured, they are very much meant for you.

In our search for completeness, again I want to remind you that everything you ever need to be perfectly at peace within your heart and to feel completely happy and content lay in your soul at this very moment. They have been there from the moment of your birth; though dormant, I assure you I see them within you. Once you know where to look and how to change your perspective of life, they will literally spring forth and change your life. I have experienced this for myself, and also know others who have done the same. While it takes patience, it is a reward well worth your efforts.

The lesson here is to begin *today* in looking nearby for the subtle energies that a positive attitude and determined spirit can bring into your world. Your answers are not far off, in some magical land. They do not lie in any particular person, relationship or place. They do not lie off in another life, or in another day of your life. What you seek is close—so very, very, close. This is one of the great mysteries I want to uncover for you. Uncovering your soul and truly understanding your world and your place in it is truly a remarkable experience. If you have been waiting for your answers to appear, they will not get any closer than the words on these pages that have been revealed to you. It all begins with an understanding of the self.

In understanding the concept of the Tao, we no longer listen to the small self, which is the selfish voice that calls out in our hearts for worldly needs.

"I want true love to be happy!"

"I want a great career!"

"I deserve so much more than what I have!"

It never ceases to stop. Learn instead to listen to the subtle energies, which the universe sends out to us in an unending stream of positive events and coincidences. It all begins by learning to detach ourselves from our complicated lives and begin sitting down and absorbing the universe, with your ears, your eyes, and every one of your senses. There is no greater lesson to teach this than solitude. You must learn to connect to the great truth that flows through every turn in the river of life. It surrounds you daily, in a million manifestations. Your confusion is caused by your detachment from it. In solitude we find another key to life.

We search for these keys all of our lives. Sometimes we try them in the wrong doors, and discard them. In understanding the Tao, we find that life is all about timing. If you understand this concept, try the key of solitude once again in your door. This time, it just may open for you.

I want to impart to you the perception that seeking change for yourself and understanding the Tao are not common goals for most people in life. I know it can seem rather solitary at times. Once begun, it is a path we must complete. You will feel it in your heart if you have been chosen.

There is yet another interesting popular film I would like to bring into focus now—*The Matrix*. In this movie, the lead character Neo knows he is different. In the following scene, Morpheus attempts to explain to Neo about the world that he had always known was not reality. In the movie, a computer program designed by machines that now ruled the earth provided a kind of electronic blindfold for all the humans, and the darkness of what had become of the earth was hidden from their senses, and humans were slaves to this electronic blindfold. A very few people had escaped this deception, and once free, tried to find others like themselves, and begin planting seeds for a new future.

Morpheus: "What you know you can't explain. But you feel it. You've felt it your entire life. That there's something wrong with the world. You don't know what it is but it's there, like a splinter in your mind driving you mad. It is this feeling that has brought you to me. Do you know what I'm talking about?"

Neo: "The Matrix?"

Many Taoists know what Morpheus is talking about. The Matrix is the blindfold that keeps the humans from seeing their real world in this movie. Desire and human needs are the blindfolds that keep our fellow man from experiencing the Tao. Here we share a common vision. With no illusions to hold him, a Taoist leads men to what has been lost. They feel the world within your world. Describing it is very difficult, but *The Matrix* has some very close parallels.

Morpheus: "Have you ever had a dream, Neo, that you were so sure was real? What if you were unable to wake from that dream? How would you know the difference between the dream world and the real world?"

Indeed. How would we know? The reality of our daily world seems very genuine, and it is. Our senses tell us so. Then why do the fruits of man seem so hollow, and the rewards we seek seem so shallow and empty? There is something missing, and we know it. We search endlessly, and in our own subconscious we make decisions to forge our happiness. But it never seems to come together for very long.

Neo and the Taoist share a certain revelation. Upon mastering their skills they both see the unique and genuine patterns that make up everything that is around them. Everything makes sense. In one of the final scenes, Neo can actually see the millions of numbers streaming through every object that makes up the electronic dream they are in. The binary numbers make up the illusion that man has accepted as reality. The Taoist also sees the truth. He knows the patterns of life, and allows himself to flow with them. By listening to the subtle energies, he strengthens his understanding and aligns himself with a force he now not only feels, but sees in all of his daily travels.

Both Neo and the Taoist move seamlessly through their surroundings and are free from the bonds that would hold them. The difference here is that Neo himself is just an actor in a movie. The Taoist lives within each of us. The choice to become is determined by your level of awareness, discipline and dedication. Once you start putting the pieces together, you become driven to see the whole picture.

Morpheus: "I'm trying to free your mind, Neo, but I can only show you the door, you're the one that has to walk through it."

The ancient Chinese masters had learned to walk through the door of mere knowledge and understanding. What they found on the other side was a world much deeper than any you could imagine. Here they learned about the Tao, and embraced all that it would teach them. Only with reluctance would the master take on a student. The student must be sincere, and show his sincerity in willing to enter the world within his world. It is a personal calling that drives us to seek that door. Only we have the ability to walk through it.

As we continue our walk in my garden, I would like to pass on to you at this point a very deep and personal message. I have known my entire life that I was different than those around me. I would look at myself in the mirror and ask myself what it was; I looked the same, yet I have felt so very different from my companions. I have always "fit in" wherever I went, with an abundance of friends and well-being. Yet I always seemed to walk away with an emptiness that I really did not fit in. What was it I was feeling? It was not unhappiness or misery. I have always been well adjusted. It was something intangible, and

I could never put my finger on it. Objects, events, and goals that brought most people satisfaction I found strangely empty and indifferent to. I succeeded at what ever I applied myself to, it just wasn't adding up.

When I entered the ocean that is the Tao, it all came together for me. It has been my destiny to follow its path. It connects me to a greater source that I forever have felt in my soul, but did not know how to recognize. My true purpose was one of service to every human I meet. Only here can I be true to myself, and feel complete and whole. It really was a difference of perspective. A Taoist has such a unique vision of his world; it cannot be viewed through conventional eyes. When I arrived at the total revelation of my spiritual destination, it all became so overwhelmingly clear. I too have passed beyond that door, and have entered into an existence so beautiful it defies description. Not all are ready to enter. My goal is to help those that seek the door beyond mere knowledge and understanding, find it. As they approach, I merely pull them through!

While there have been so very few companions in my life that share this same understanding and gift, I understand now who I am, know my true purpose, and take comfort in comprehending the entire picture of our existence. Though I dream one day of a world filled with humans that share these gifts, for now, it is a solitary path. A Taoist plants many seeds in his life. I live to know that one day these plains will become an Eden. It is all one man can do.

In the following poem "The Shadow", I capture for you my own feelings of the Tao and how I feel about the experience.

The Shadow

The world that I watch in absentee
and this shadow I chase into ascendancy
I turn to find once more it follows me.

So what have I learned, and where shall I find
the master of the voice that whispers from far behind
the crevices so dark, and deep within my mind.

The question appears, and the answer I fear
lies in the weight I have carried, deep within my soul.
The door that is locked, the half within the whole.

There is a mission, a call, a want and a need
to know all that I am is no more than a seed.

That a forest may grow, and it could start with only me
From the chasm I peer into my darkened destiny;
critical mass, I leap into the mystery.

Morning finds me not in the man you've known,
but in a world from which that seed has grown.

I now hear the shadow, and know from which it came
that it and I are one and the same.

JR

As I have found my purpose and understand my mission in life, so too will you. It will happen at the right time, and for the right reason. It always does. If we actively pursue our happiness with a correct and open mind, we may arrive there so much sooner!

In our lives, we seek out companionship and comfort from our fellow man. We must also find the balance to this in our more solitary moments. The Yang of our daily active lives must also be balanced by the Yin of a quiet and subtle evening. In taking the time to just sit down and talk to yourself, you gain some insight into your true motivations in life. In learning to leave even your own thoughts out of this process and in letting your mind be still and quiet, you may hear and feel the subtle energies that the Tao flows continually in your direction. This is not loneliness or separation. Quite the contrary, here you are joining the Source of all things.

I want you to leave this chapter with the understanding that in our search for our spiritual destinies, embracing the inner rooms of our mind through the use of solitude in time opens other doors we need to examine. It is the cloth you use to wipe the dirt from the window of life we continually try and peer through. Instead of looking through the window and watching an existence you long to join, it is a key to unlocking the door that will forever allow you entry into a world you have only yet begun to imagine.

In our most quiet and personal moments, let us know that within a mind of silence, valuable gifts await for us to open. The subtle energies cannot enter a busy mind. Now that you have an understanding of their purpose, you will welcome them as all of our spiritual teachers and great sages have learned. In the stillness of the night, or in a quiet day on my porch, I have learned to welcome them, that they may cleanse my mind, and show me once again, I hold the secret to life within my arms. While the passer by may think I am being lazy, he couldn't be farther from the truth. In my stillness, I am letting the universe take a stroll through my mind. The subtle energies dance ever so silent, and with them the calmness and understanding of a hidden world invades my senses. This is the great secret of our sages. In these very pages, I give it to you now. Let it be the critical mass, the catalyst in your ever-changing world.

The feelings I have stirred within you, and in the lesson of solitude we hear the silent message that whispers ever so softly in our minds; *There is so much more to who I am!* From our night on the shore, we have found this truth. As we leave again in the morning on the great lake of life, let us remember this evening, that we may return to it again and again, and understand more completely, that an entire immense power continually flows to us, through the path opened by solitude. Here we find that an open mind frees the open heart, and the open heart now beats in time to the song of the universe.

Dancing by Myself

It's so different;
    the sounds I hear,
        the air I breathe,
           and yet it seems so clear.

It's like the universe is reaching in,
    the one you never knew,
        and it's passing now,
           from me deep into you.

And all I can do is take it all in,
    and shape it for you to see,
        the beauty of who you are,
           and all we're meant to be.

Joseph Roggenbeck

I know in time
    that it waits for me,
        and I'll find that place
            that I am destined to be.

For now I'll just keep dancing by myself,
    it's coming through so clear,
        surrendering it all to the music
        that only I can hear.

JR

Fear

The foundation of our drive to spirituality can be discovered in many places. When we search for our answers in life, there is usually some compelling event or tragedy that has entered our lives. When we try to rationalize these events, an age-old emotion rises from within our thoughts and grips us in its jaws—fear. The unknown is its home, and our minds become its prey. While we struggle to drive it out, invariably it returns. Can we really have any control over this beast? The answer to this is found within the other side of the equation—faith. Our journey thus far has led us to understand that knowledge for its own sake is limited. When we apply the wisdom of the Tao, we may find a more complete answer.

Wisdom can be found in many documents, by many authors. In the Bible, the first letter of John reveals to us some words that we may all benefit from, no matter what faith we serve.

> "There is no fear in love; perfect love drives out all fear. So then, love has not been made perfect in anyone who is afraid, because fear has to do with punishment."
>
> *1 John 4:18*

Here, John points out so eloquently to us that pure and true love transcends all fear. If we truly have faith in our partners in life, our Gods, and yes even ourselves, then we have discovered the foundation and solitude in our souls that will strengthen us to a level where fear may not enter our lives. We become transparent, and there is no place for fear to enter. There are times in our lives where we literally have to make a leap of faith. There are no guarantees, no safety nets, and no promise of success. But we reach a point in our journeys where there are no other options. In these dark moments of our existence, we must reach inside ourselves and discover that hidden strength that lies in all of us—total faith. Here fear cannot enter. In understanding our faith systems, we must proceed with full commitment. Whichever faith system you follow, follow it in its fullness. Only then will you receive the incredible strength that pure faith has to offer—absolute fearlessness.

> "Be it life or death, we crave only reality. If we are really dying, let us hear the rattle in our throats and feel the cold in our extremities: if we are alive, let us go about our business."
>
> *Henry David Thoreau*

Here, Thoreau very bluntly tells us, we either must choose to go on, or lay down our lives. In the movie *Shawshank Redemption* based on a story by Stephen King, there is a similar quote, yet even starker in contrast.

"I guess it comes down to a simple choice, really. Get busy living or get busy dying."

The message here is that no matter how dark our lives get, we really must find a way to carry on. There is no other choice for us to make.

In the following poem *Within,* I wanted to open a window for you to travel into my past. With the influence of unstoppable willpower, it is possible to conquer any obstacle or challenge of fate. Though fear is powerful, it can only be as strong as the strength that we give it. Once I hold it in proper perspective, it holds no power over me. Once again we find perspective has the power to conquer every challenge we may meet. For those fighting with their own personal challenges, this verse is for you.

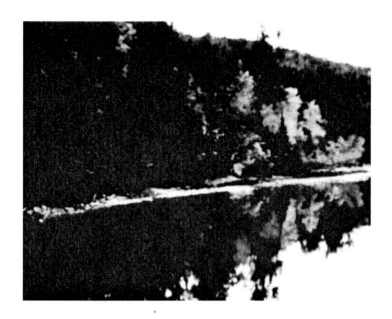

Within

Today I free myself, from my fears entwined,
my faith the light, the shadow defined.
In the breeze that wanders freely, a stranger calls;
Hope whispers quietly from behind these walls.

In the storm I feared, the face I see,
was always that of destiny,
and rainbows I held in certainty,
were layered in shades of mediocrity.

This door that holds me I find unreal
the truth before which did my sorrow conceal.
Will of mind, or gate of steel,
the stronger which did time reveal?

Fate has called, the hour is here,
from the darkness behind me to the light so clear.
Faith and fear, into this scale I weigh,

the stronger which, I cannot say.

Light appears, and within I see,
a cameo of who I used to be.
Through the mist of change
the man I've sought my life to find,
was wrapped within the darkness of my mind.

JR

We all handle our fear in many different ways. In order for us to overcome our fears, we must define them, that we can put a light into the darkness. Once we look at our fears objectively, their hold over us is lessened. Some fears pass, once the crisis is past us. We look back and remember how terrified or worried we were over something very personal and close to us. But the morning light of a new day that shines on us once the moment has passed brings with it a relaxing solitude; we made it. Within the race of our lives we have cleared another hurdle.

But what of the hurdle we do not clear? What do we do when life has taken us down, and that hurdle still stands before us? These are our true challenges, and in that offsetting balance, the weakness of our faith, gives way to the strength of our fears. Somehow, each of us must find a spiritual solution to help make us stronger, that we may get past that obstacle that lies before us.

In my youth, I was not a particularly great religious student. But of all the teachings I had been through, I always held one in particular with a very close and personal interest. I have found comfort in its words, and though it is a popular reading, I would be remiss not to include it here for you now. I find it is timeless, and that it really exemplifies true faith. Faith is the master of all fear. You either have one or the other, you cannot believe in both. It is truly a weighted scale—the more on one side of the balance, the less on the other side. In the twenty-third Psalm, it drives this point home for us.

The Lord is my Shepherd;
I shall not want.
He maketh me to lie down in green pastures:
He leadeth me beside the still waters.
He restoreth my soul: He leadeth me in the paths of
righteousness for His name's sake.
Yea, though I walk through the valley of the shadow of
death, I will fear no evil:
For thou art with me;
Thy rod and Thy staff they comfort me
in the presence of mine enemies:
Thou anointest my head with oil;
my cup runneth over.
Surely goodness and mercy shall follow me
All the days of my life:
and I will dwell in the house of the Lord forever.

"For thou art with me." I find this quite a powerful statement, with an underlying strength that surfaces in our minds. Knowing we are not alone on our journey is very comforting isn't it? Two can face what one cannot. Whether it is a friend or a God, we tend to survive better with a little help. When you are backed into your next corner, reach out. There is always someone nearby that will take your hand. For that is the way of the Tao, always supplying to us what we need, when we need it.

"The only thing we have to fear is fear itself."

Franklin D. Roosevelt

Faith and fear are opposite ends in the polar equation of life. Faith is bright, all knowing, strong and illuminating. It is the Yang of this balance. Fear is dark, unknown and weakening, the Yin of the cycle. They are intrinsically tied together. A little of each is born in their cycles. Together, we see how the cycle brings into our lives, adversity and challenge. It is in the eye of the beholder, which is greater, and what he will do with it when it arrives.

It is with a clear mind that the sage walks with no fear. She does so by trusting entirely in the cycles of life. What is born will die, what dies will be reborn. This is the cycle of the Tao. By living her life entirely in detachment, there is no desire, thus no ache in her heart. Whatever comes her way is accepted, both good and bad. In her beauty that is the Tao radiating in her reflection, what does she have to ever fear in her life?

When a country is in harmony with the Tao,
The people are simple and honest.
When a country goes counter to the Tao,
Men are cruel and ruthless.

Seeking desires, you will find fear.
Seeking fortune, you will find misfortune.
The sage has no desires, no riches, and thus no enemies.

Seeking only enlightenment
He leaves the human condition far below
And is forever safe.

From chapter 46 of the Tao Te Ching

Here, Lao Tzu directs our attention to perception. If a man perceives a threat, real or imagined, he disconnects himself from the Tao, by the mere act of giving the fear power over him. Nothing can create anger or fear within you. Only you allow these feelings to take control, and thus they grow to an obstacle within your heart. If I imagine the worst that could happen from a fear that enters my mind, and plan for that outcome, does it not reduce somewhat in magnitude in my mind? So here, we see that perspective not only gives structure to the relative size of our fears, but also can eliminate them by the mere act of practicing the most basic Taoist principles.

If I genuinely come to accept that good and bad hold equal value, then what is there to ever fear? I am smiling right now, thinking again of how this concept is so simple to view, yet difficult to grasp. It is no illusion my friend. The illusion lives in your current belief system that we can only accept good things in our lives. Because no one has taught this to you before, you are reluctant to believe. Once you understand the material in this text, you will truly be the great sage, one who may grasp all of life's events, and accept them all. Here, there never is disappointment, sadness, desire, or worst of all, fear. Fear is merely a shadow that man has allowed to creep and hide inside the corners of his mind. Any event that may hold pain or suffering, we allow fear to grow, and perpetuate its control over our judgment, and thus our lives. If I accept that all of life is part of a great cycle, and within that are hidden aspects of good and bad, all of which I cannot control, what is left for me to do, except to understand them and limit their influence over me? It is only our reaction to life that we may control. All else are shadows for us to chase.

When that little voice returns to you this week, tell him, "Small self, I now understand your powers over me, and thus I am free of them." It is quite a grip our small self has clasped over our lives. We have allowed this to happen by giving it the power to control us. If you really want to eliminate fear in your life, stop listening to the small self, and listen instead to the subtle energies of the Tao. In its own pure understanding and beauty, fear has never entered. What a truly great traveler you will become! This basic concept, once grasped, can allow a man to pass beyond where all before him could not.

In accepting the bad within the good, and the good within the bad, no enemy can strike you, for there is no place for his weapon to enter. With no conflict, life and your perceptions of it will come to a new and magnificent understanding. Your future now has as many options as your mind can comprehend. A peaceful mind is bright and sharp, the jewel of the Tao shining through. When we meet on the path of life, I will know this for the truth when I look into your eyes. The eyes of a clear mind shine brilliantly, a window to the peace that lies within.

The Kid I Once Knew

In your lifetime up to this point, when was the most carefree happy time where you felt the days went on forever? For many of us, that period would have to be our youth, most likely our pre-teenage years. I was ten years old. I can remember getting up in the morning, running outside, feeling the warm sunshine, slipping on my old mud soaked tennis shoes and running over to my best friend's house. We would grab our fishing poles and head full speed out to the lake. The whole time we used to laugh and joke and explore our world, with so many options to choose from, it seemed a thousand summers would never be enough time to do everything we planned.

We didn't want to miss a thing, so we would skip our meals, and hold mom off while we ran out to pick up our bikes. It seemed our clothing was not that important either. Hey, if we wore it in the lake, that was really the same thing as washing it, wasn't it? At night, our families would gather around the campfire and we would all tell stories about what we had done during the day. More laughter would always follow when we got done with our tall tales. We would be so dirty, my mom would make us rinse off in the lake before we could get a bath! When bedtime came, sleep would follow so naturally it was like turning off a light switch. I remember lying in bed and giggling to myself about some humorous event we had created during the day. I would hurry up and go to sleep so tomorrow would arrive. Everyday was like Christmas to us. When morning came, we were off and running again. We didn't have any money. We lived hand to mouth every year. We never had any fancy toys. Our summer home was a trailer. It didn't matter to us. The world was ours, and there was no limit on how much fun we could bag, and we took it all.

Time waits for no man though. My teenage years arrived, and with it, so many new problems. My needs and desires had changed overnight. The world seemed so different to me, but I could not exactly tell you when it had changed. It just did somehow, when I wasn't looking I guess. I can remember looking back at that time wondering, "Where did it all go?"

Teenage years are typically very polarizing, with periods of brief happiness followed by extended times of depression and searching. I was searching for where to put all of the square pegs when all I could find was round holes. As I began looking for my answers in that period, I can remember wondering where it all would end. Why couldn't I be back just fishing with my old pal again? It didn't seem very fair. Working was no fun at all. I didn't mind hard work; it just took so much time! Then there were girls, and I had no clue about how I was supposed to handle that one.

How confusing it all was. It was so frustrating to have so many problems with no easy answers. I longed for much simpler times. A walk down to the old fishing hole was in order. I arrived to discover a subdivision had sprouted and staked out the entire area for itself; nothing but boats and docks and rafts with fences and "No Trespassing" signs. In that moment I learned the lesson of never looking back. "Enjoy each moment while you are there." I remember thinking. "Because when the hole is fished out, it just isn't fun anymore." Sometimes we can mark a period of our life by a certain event. That was mine, and I will never forget it. Solace was my only companion as I made one of the longest walks I have ever had.

Then I met my girlfriend, finished high school, college, marriage, began working for a living, raising children, it all happened so fast. We were really happy. Such a perfect match, and so much in love, we had it all. Just as it was all finally coming together again, tragedy struck. Remember the old saying, "Into every life some rain must fall." Well, it was a hurricane for us.

A minor car accident had triggered a dormant autoimmune disorder in my wife. Things began changing rapidly for us. Roles had become reversed. With her unable to work, my job became paramount. Our children were still fairly young at the time. Literally hundreds of hours spent at doctors, clinics, labs and hospitals ate away at our once peaceful existence. What a dark time in our lives. While pushing myself as hard as I knew how to, it was just not enough. The years began to pass. One day I just sat down and told to no one around me, "I give up."

I was angry at the world. Nothing in my mind could reconcile these events to me. I watched her suffer so much, with no hope or progress. It had become the most frustrating and unbearable thing to experience. We were both good hard working honest people who had lived by every law know to God and man. That didn't seem to matter. Adversity had taken us in its relentless grip. The rain was coming down hard.

My nature is one of being passive, but underneath that also lays a fighter. When I decide to do something, look out. There isn't an army or a wall big enough to stop me. But here I was up against the biggest monster I had ever seen, and nothing I tried could even make a dent in it, and it was growing. My biggest fear was that it would consume me, and with it my wife. I finally got mad enough to leave my depression in the background. I have never lost at any thing I had ever taken on—not once—and I wasn't going to start now. But I had to find a way to win. My faith system I was raised with was fine for everyday things, but it had failed me, or I had failed it, I am still not sure which. There remained nagging questions unanswered about God in my mind. It seemed I could always put those off until some more important time. Well, it was time now, and I knew it. It was do or die, sink or swim, and I had been treading water for quite some time.

I stumbled upon Taoism, or it stumbled upon me. Again the power of synchronicity quietly showed itself. Finally my answers started coming. It was a tidal wave of understanding unleashed and running through my body. That fuzzy picture of life I had been viewing suddenly became crystal clear. Everything made sense to me now! There was no limit to what I could take on. I had received immortality. It was a gift from the Gods to me. I used it to reshape myself. I changed my attitudes, my goals and with it my life.

Through it all, I had climbed the highest mountain; I had endured the storm of a lifetime. No man can experience the depth of that misery and the pain of being stripped down to the core of his basic soul without being forever changed by it. Through it all, I looked back at my wife, as she had been watching my transformation. I had discovered that through it all, my biggest anger was for myself, the things that affected me. My own selfish desires had caused my own unhappiness. When I finally got down to basics, it was really all the changes and sacrifices that I knew I had to face that was really the issue. I had seen the enemy, and it was me.

When I came back to where I had left off in my life, there was my wife, waiting patiently for me to return. While my own metamorphosis was painful and self-imposed, my wife had never experienced transformation – her wings have carried her since birth. She was a natural Taoist and I had missed it the whole time! She never has a concern about herself. She only offers help whenever possible, every day with never any demands. Whatever comes her way she takes it all in and smiles the best she can. She accepts her diseases with a shrug, and lives her life like the calm surface of the lake in the morning. It is her body that is sick, certainly not her mind. Side by side we have always walked in step, in perfect synchronicity.

When I had found the truth that the Tao had revealed to me, the scattered pieces to my puzzle of life began flying to me, putting themselves in perfect order with no hammers needed. "Why had this taken so long to happen?" I asked myself. The old fishing hole was back, and I had suddenly become ten years old again. It took the misery of my existence to its lowest form for me to find the faith system that would let me be at peace with my world. In this I began to rebuild myself to a much deeper man than I ever could have been before. Again we see the lesson of the good within the bad. At the time I was too close to it to understand. So the endless cycle of the Tao has shown itself again. Once we know what to look for and recognize the signs, everything will come together, and so it has for me.

As a child, we have little responsibility. Everything is new and shiny. Our world is very much about exploring. Taking it all in every day becomes an endless joy. A cardboard box can hold endless hours of entertainment. The toy that came in it waits patiently for its turn. In this period of innocence lie many secrets that become lost as we grow. The once supple and flexible child becomes rigid and hardened. Is it any wonder that our happiness leaves us as we grow old? Here Lao Tzu again puts this lesson in perfect perspective for us.

Men are born gentle and weak.
When he dies, he is hard and inflexible.
Young plants are tender and full of life.
At their death they are withered and dry.

Therefore the rigid and unbending,
Is the follower of death.
The soft and yielding
Is the follower of life.

When the wind blows hard,
The tree that stands fast is overcome.
The flexible tree bends
And thus survives.

Chapter 76 of the Tao Te Ching

I would like to leave this chapter with a few simple thoughts. Though we can never be children again, there are some basic lessons we can keep. I have started a list, but I am sure you can add to it.

❖ There is a time to work and a time to play. It is OK to have your work become playtime, but never let your playtime become work.

❖ Toys are fun when we enjoy them, but get broken, lost, or taken away when we don't share or make time for others to be with us. - All things in moderation.

❖ No one likes a whiner or a complainer. - If you want solitude, this is the surest way.

❖ We build sandcastles in the summer and snowmen in the winter. - There is a correct time for everything. When the timing is right, things will happen naturally.

❖ Diving with a loose swimsuit will always make people laugh, no matter how old you are.

❖ The sooner I say, "I'm sorry", the sooner I can come out of the corner. - Let us honor our partners in life. They deserve your honesty and humility.

❖ Giving a big smile is the best way to get one back.

❖ Nothing melts a cold moment like a warm hug.

❖ I will always be around for grandpa when he forgets who he is. I would never want him to feel lost. – Honor thy father and thy mother.

❖ Stick up for your friends, even when his enemies are bigger than you. Win or lose, we will stick together. - Besides, mom has ice cream and Band Aids if we lose.

❖ It's OK to play make believe, but in the end, I just want to be me.

❖ When you can make a nun laugh and avoid a punishment, truly you have been given a reprieve from God. - A good sense of humor will take you far.

❖ When the neighbors bring you a new Etch A Sketch, it really doesn't matter why you are in the hospital and your legs are paralyzed. - Learn to make do with the simple things in life.

❖ When the sun is out and I'm outside with it, we are going to have a great day. - Life is all about attitude.

❖ It's OK when your old fishing hole closes. We can go find another one. It might just have bigger fish! – There is nothing more constant than change. Those that adapt, learn to endure.

You are never too old to dance in the rain; you just get a few more odd looks when you are older. It's OK to be yourself, take pride in your ability to be independent. Celebrate who you are. Leave before the cops show up.

My daughter put my personality in perfect perspective one day. She has a very quick wit and I have always admired her openness.

"Dad, it's like you were the kid who never grew up!"

I thought about this statement for a moment and finally replied to her.

"I hope I never do!"

I sincerely believe a youthful attitude keeps us young and open-minded. Some of the most fascinating people I have ever met had this unique quality. It is our ability to constantly be flexible, happy and unbiased that lets our attitude shine through every hole in the fence of solitude, that all may peer through and long to join us in our dance of life.

Joseph Roggenbeck

For Today

For today, I leave my worries,
in a box upon the shelf
Only to meet a stranger
I used to call myself

For today, I think I shall try her on
my mind becomes so clear
Let us embrace this day we have
before you disappear

For today, we will watch the clouds
to see a young hawk fly
My shadow races down below
as I watch within his eye

For today, we will rest upon
a blanket woven of living thread
and listen to our friend the wind
and all that he has said

For today, we will be the sun
and warm the earth below
To feel life unfold itself
this gift we now bestow

For today, I found I've missed you so
this friendship long denied
the box I leave unto itself
the darkness trapped inside-

JR

Chariot of Life

Your body is your "vehicle" in this crazy world. It takes you where you want to go. You take care of it, provide for it, and preserve its safety. When our time on earth expires, we leave this behind to continue in the cosmic recycle program of the universe. Don't get too attached to it. It is subject to disease, decay, and a very frustrating aging process. It doesn't define who you are. It is a mere physical representation of who you display to the world. Did you pick your features out? Did anyone ask your input on its creation? No. So why waste time and energy trying to redefine, remodel and accessorize it? Are you not beautiful by the natural system that created all of us? You are perfect just the way you are. Keeping our body maintained is important. Just don't identify it with who you are. It is a physical shell that holds your mind. It will grow, age, and heal naturally. It is merely a part of the natural cycle of the universe. Learn to accept this.

> "Every man is the builder of a temple, called his body, to the God he worships, after a style purely his own, nor can he get off hammering marble instead. We are all sculptors and painters and our material is our own flesh and blood."

> *Henry David Thoreau*

Defined by nature, your body has natural needs. The needs to sleep, eat, and proliferate are the three most basic human urges. These are to keep the species in circulation. In moderation, all fit nicely into the human model. Any desire to consciously elevate the body's requirements to self-gratuitous levels will result in an unnatural balance. We are naturally inclined to external addictions as well. Smoking, drugs and alcohol; these distractions are as endless as the stars. All represent negative energy in your body. This imbalance leads to disharmony in your well-being.

"Unhappiness comes from having a body.
Without a body, how could there be unhappiness?"

Lao Tzu

In my search for happiness, I wanted total control in my life. No crutches and no excuses. By looking inside myself and watching my fellow humans, I arrived at one very obvious truth. Drugs, alcohol and smoking are all forms of external addictions that we allow to stream into our bodies, filling a perceived hole in our personalities that we externally substitute these damaging habits with. By accepting these habits in our lives, we have given them control over a portion of who we are. As we come to understand our weaknesses and recognize the subconscious purpose of our actions, we begin to bring them to a conscious level and reduce our dependency on them. In our insecurity, we have chosen to hide behind these destructive elements and the false security they give us. Be strong enough to say to yourself, "I do not need these to feel happy or complete." They only detract from who you are, and put your health at risk. These are all self-destructive behaviors that we can control, if we have the strength to make the conscious decision to leave them behind. With a healthier body, you will find it easier to connect to the subtle energies that are hidden in our daily lives. In simplifying our lives, we achieve balance and contentment. Never let an addiction separate you from the Tao. It is a distraction we can do without.

"I know this, but I just can't stop myself!" We all have heard this response. I have one comment for you here. In our lives, we have certain weaknesses in our own self-confidence. In letting these addictions continue their destructive effects on our bodies and our minds, we are giving in to the pressures of modern life and society. We are in effect saying, "I am too weak to overcome this!"

There is no addiction that exists that you cannot overcome. It is determination and willpower that will conquer these challenges. You will need much more of both to achieve true happiness and contentment that are the rewards of following the Tao. You must begin by letting negative energy *out* of your body, and stop putting it *in*. You must be the best advocate for yourself; no one else is going to do it for you. Learn to be independent and strong. Tell yourself today as you look into the mirror, that you welcome happiness and peace in your life, and that it all begins with no external addictions.

It all comes down to control. Either I control my body, my emotions and my future health, or I let some drug do it for me. Drugs have no conscience and no master. They answer to no one. If we do not take control of these, then we are their slaves, for they have become our master. In order to effect true contentment and positive change in our lives, we must first take control of our bodies. If my body and mind are under the influence of an addiction, the connection to the Tao cannot be found. We have become too dependent on our desires, and fall victim to their control over us.

The power of change is the most incredible force in the universe, and yet it lies within your very mind. Flip the switch. Yield the sword. Only you can do it. For yourself and all around you in your life, you can say, "I am strong, and I leave my crutch behind me."

Respect this gift of flesh that has been given to us to enjoy. It is the chariot we have been given to carry us from this experience into the next. If you truly seek more control over your life, then let it begin with your own flesh and blood. When we begin to find peace within our bodies, then surely our minds cannot be far behind.

Joseph Roggenbeck

In Sickness and in Health

If you enjoy the gift of good health, please consider yourself fortunate. In our entire lives we will endure times when we will not be so lucky. It is human nature to believe that it is a given right that we are entitled to good health. Let me assure you, this can change literally in your next heartbeat.

When we are healthy, life is good. We can focus on our pleasures and do things that are creative; paint a picture, write a poem, or sing a song you have just written. Watching the world outside, such a beautiful and open place where all our happiness and dreams flow, it is hard to believe that another world coexists in sharp contrast to the one we have always known.

Poor health will bring a new perspective. Your world around you becomes restructured, boundaries change, and you feel a cold wind blowing. It can be a very dark and frightening place. There are no rules here. Time becomes suspended. With your health compromised and the future uncertain, the path ahead is lined with doctors, hospitals and treatments. Your friends will act differently towards you. Conversations will now be strangely awkward. Your physical appearance will change right before your very eyes. Tasks you once performed a million times will now become a Herculean effort. Survival is now your number one priority. You now belong to *the fallen.*

The fallen know who they are. They are the walking wounded, the undiagnosed, and the ones searching for answers. They want to know how to get back to the road they were on. It seemed so long ago that they once traveled that road. Was it really a dream, or some strange alternate reality that they once were healthy? It has been so long. Endless hours are spent searching the Internet. Lab results are cross-examined and catalogued. You await your next CAT scan results like a gladiator staring at the emperor. Will it be "Live!" or "Die!" You cannot stand the waiting. When will it all end? Sleep becomes your only escape. This is the only refuge to be found from the tragic world that has encircled you.

The fallen suffer the indignation of many uncaring health professionals and insurance companies. They endure endless tests looking for answers. Injections and medications wreak havoc on their bodies. Negative reactions from the drugs bring on more drugs, sending them into an endless downward spiral of strangeness and sensations changing their metaphysical existence.

Society reacts very strangely to *the fallen*. Many will come to support you at first. The gifts, the flowers, the phone calls, and the visitors all wishing you well. This is where the separation begins. People you have trusted your whole life seem remote and become unattached. They stop looking at you, not wanting to meet your eyes. Their contact becomes less frequent; they are noticeably uncomfortable around you now. Slowly they begin to fade away.

Fear has driven them away. The reality of your situation has hit a little too close to home. This could happen to *them*. Besides, they have busy lives. What else can be done? It is their inability to reach out and put your needs before their own that drives them away. Don't blame them; they are only reacting the only way that they have ever known. Life is a strange teacher. The lessons come in no certain order, but rest assured, they will all come to everyone. That is a fact of the human condition.

Conversely, people you barely had known or even strangers will reach out to you. They will perform great acts of kindness and compassion. They will become your strength, your support, and even your heroes. It is a beautiful contrast, a rainbow in the storm. Oh the balance of the universe in action! Times like these will demonstrate how all things balance out in the end. We just need to look for them and understand the signs when they make themselves known.

Joseph Roggenbeck

Talking to Trees -

Many years ago, I moved into my current home. Being a new construction, there was much landscaping to do. I began with one acre of sand, and have since transformed it into a pleasing yard that was completely of my own hands and on a strict budget as well. I began with a few existing trees that were on the property. In one corner of the lot grew a beautiful pine. It was about ten feet in height and very full and green. As you approached the house, it was waiting there, greeting all that took notice.

While my landscaping was coming together, my life was coming apart. My wife and I continued on as the years ticked by, struggling with her disease and all of the challenges we both faced with handling it. It had become overwhelming for me. There was no solution and no comfort for us, just a continued daily struggle to survive. Day-by-day, week after week we rebuilt the best life we knew how. With what resources we could find, we held on to each other as tight as we could, but still she suffered mercifully. Watching a loved one in the prime of their life slowly slip away from you is the most draining of life's tragedies that one can experience. Here I realized how delicately we had traversed our lives, unaware that the hand of fate we walked upon was merely a tight rope, and we must carefully watch every step we take. How much I had taken for granted.

I went outside to gather my thoughts one day. As I toured the yard seeking gratification from nature and all the comfort within her beauty, my eyes came to rest on my favorite tree in my yard once again. I could not believe what I saw. Every needle on every branch lay now upon the ground! Overnight this tree had died! I shook my head as I examined it. It seemed as though everything in my life was suffering. I was very distressed as I walked away. The world I was witnessing at this point was a very dark one indeed. The tree was just one more highlight for my darkened attitude.

As the weeks passed by, a neighbor commented that I would have to replace my dead tree. "It's not dead!" I shouted, "It's sleeping!" We both chuckled as I turned back and touched the dead branches. Maybe she was just sleeping. Stranger things have happened, right? I closed my eyes and imagined the roots, still alive, gathering strength. I pictured it green and brilliant, bigger and more beautiful then ever. Maybe it would come back to life. I would wait and see.

Months passed, and now it was autumn. It was time to cut the grass again. As I rounded the house and headed for the yard, something caught my eye. It was just outside my senses, but the urge to follow it was strong, so I succumbed to my instinct and continued looking in the direction of my dead tree. Was it a trick of light? No, there were new green buds forming on the branches! Not just a few, but the entire tree! It was a feeling of revelation that passed through me. I knew it was just a tree, but it was *my* tree. I had not given up on it, and we were both rewarded with the gift of continued life. What a dramatic and symbolic event to happen when I so desperately needed a positive sign in my life.

I had been reading about Taoism and was trying to understand how it all fit into the model of my life. With the tree I had learned a lesson about the cycle of life and events that were beyond our control. I also learned to greatly appreciate all of my other trees that grew in their own silent grandeur. As I looked back at my wife who had struggled outside and made it into a chair on the deck, a new world had quietly opened through a door in my mind that I never knew was there. Life was so much a balance. It can be so beautiful! That is the way of the Tao. Take it all in, every second of every day. For one day the needles will drop. That also is the way of the Tao. This was my lesson that day. We must celebrate not only what is seen, but also all of which remains unseen.

But that is not the end to my little story.

The years passed by. I continued to study the Tao and observe it in all of my daily travels. To say that I had overcome my former self and all of my shortcomings was an understatement. I had been miraculously transformed. The power of the universe was the blood within my veins, and I really believed that I had found the secret to life. To have all of life make sense, while having total contentment with every event was the gift I had given myself. It was very much the most difficult and rewarding task I have ever taken on.

Then I was diagnosed with cancer. I reconciled within myself all of the possibilities and approaches I could take. I could not be the person I had used to know. I had come too far for that. The person I had become was strong; perhaps the strongest I have known. In every person I meet, I search their eyes for that same strength. I knew I was mentally prepared for anything that the world could throw my way. In this person I could take on the cancer.

I walked outside and wandered for a while, drifting in thought as I formed a battle plan in my mind. The sun was out and it was a beautiful fall day. The birds were dancing about, unconcerned with my condition. The clouds passed overhead, the intricate formations oblivious to my thoughts. Life would continue on, just as it always had. In the cycle of life, my number might just have come up. It's strange how you never can really know what you will do when faced with that weight to carry. With the power and understanding of my world around me, I found a solitude that few men can ever know. If death was here to take me on that ride into the unknown, then I was ready. I would finish this world with strength and dignity. If you truly believe that all of life continues on, in forms unknown to us here in this reality, then there is no fear. I was feeling very good about my decision and its confirmation of my beliefs. The cancer was not an enormous immovable boulder, it would be just a small stone for me, and I could surely carry that!

I stopped and looked around me to find that I had unconsciously arrived at my favorite tree. It had doubled in height since its recovery. I brushed her branches ever so softly with my hand. I thought of how my neighbor had given up on her when she appeared totally without hope.

"We will have much to talk about after I beat this cancer," I whispered. "Thank you for the lesson I have learned." I closed my eyes and imagined all of the tree's energy now flowing into my body as I touched her ever so softly. I imagined my own body responding and getting stronger. It was electrifying. When I opened my eyes, it was all so amazingly clear! I walked away from that tree with the strongest confirmation of the Tao I had yet come to know. I would be fine either way, life or death. Healthy, sick, or disabled, I could take it all on. The understanding of the Tao was a tool that had made me invincible.

The tree and I had many other secret meetings. It has been a very long road, but my cancer is now in remission. In our own ways, we had not only changed our own realities, but had given others the strength to carry on. It was not yet our time, and we both knew it. Though disease is destructive to our bodies, it is crucial to separate our physical pain from our minds. In my own sickness, I continued to find the beauty in every day, in every event and in each synchronistic manifestation of the Tao that continually flowed my way. Here I found contrast and balance to the darkness within my cancer. It could have my body, but my soul was mine to own.

In the events we daily experience, keep this perspective in your mind. Remaining centered in the face of all adversity is a victory of our *own* making. It can all begin for you here in the lesson of the tree. Though I have been one of *the fallen*, I also have become the victor. In the battle for our lives, find the warrior that lies dormant within you. Though the paths to pick up that sword are many, it can be found as easily as talking to a tree. And so it is.

Relationships

In our search for a deeper understanding of life and the rationalization of our place in the world, we recognize that we are only humans. We are not all knowing entities. We make errors, and stumble in our confusion. We fall down a lot in our learning process of life. We learn from our mistakes, and correct them so that we may enjoy a brighter future.

But we also recognize that we are not alone in this journey through life. We are surrounded by fellow travelers, all on their own journeys as well. We all travel at our own speed, in our own ways. We are climbing the mountain of life the only way we know how. The paths to our destinations are many, and ultimately we must make choices. With every choice comes a commitment. Friendships and relationships are truly very deep commitments. Marriage is the deepest commitment of all.

In our lives, we may never face a bigger challenge than forming a successful marriage. It is the ultimate sacrifice. In fulfilling our own requirements for happiness, we must balance those of another in a complex and paradoxical relationship that requires an intense commitment to develop. We know that we must accept change, both in our own views and in our spouse. Life is very much a constantly changing enigma that we try desperately to keep our arms around and maintain some sense of control. To coordinate all of these events with another in perfect synchronicity is an enormous challenge. It seldom is a perfect result. We must temper our wants with our resources. We do not always have what we need from our partners in life; rest assured though, that is a mutual experience for them as well. If we wish a truly deep experience from our marriage, then know that it must begin with ourselves. You cannot control another. You can only be a person that can be loved. The rest is up to them.

When you have compromised all you can, when you have given every ounce of strength that lays within you, and when you can honestly give all of yourself with no demands or requirements of your partner in life, only then can you say that you have given it your very best effort. It takes time for people to change. Be patient. There is much at stake here. Sometimes we must wait patiently for our partners to meet us again on the path to moving forward in our lives. Sometimes you will be the teacher, developing your spouse into a much deeper human. Sometimes you will be the student, suddenly aware that your roles have been reversed! Be aware that we have much to learn from each other.

In today's world, we have an unfortunate tendency to look at marriage as an arrangement that is to benefit us until something better comes along. It is merely a document that can be bargained away, an unfortunate experience we can walk away from. I find no honor here in this casual acceptance of a failed promise.

Every man and woman must live their lives in honor that they display the value and meaning of all the morals that we claim to support in this society. If we truly are seeking happiness, then we must temper that with patience and commitment. Life is not always an easy road. That is why we have chosen to bond ourselves to another, that we may reap the rewards of the power of two. Whether I sign a document, shake your hand, or give you a promise from my lips, it is a contract of honor and integrity. I must display and fulfill this contract that I may be true to myself and the morals I claim to value. If I cannot live by my word, then I live without morals and truth. In our vows, let us remember—"for better or worse, for richer and poorer, in sickness and in health, until death do us part."

These are not idle words to be taken lightly. We have sworn them before our God, our friends, and our families. Life is a very difficult journey. Step up and accept that you have made an irreversible commitment to your partner. The possibility of a very intense and deeply personal relationship exists in every marriage. Reach inside yourself and find whatever it takes, sacrifice everything you are and make it happen for you. It is not some magical Eden that you are swept to by the mere act of placing a ring on your hand. It is a garden you create with your partner in life. You build it plant by plant, stone by stone, over years and years of tireless work. If you and your partner's garden has grown over with weeds and vines, pick up that rake of devotion, the shovel of commitment that you have chosen, and build it to what you want to see. It is up to you what your future will be here. You must seek out new ways to engage your partner to help. These stones and trees require the strength of two to move. In the end, the garden you build will only be as beautiful as the commitment you have served in putting it all together. I firmly believe that we get out of life exactly what we put into it. Not all marriages can be saved, but we walk away from them all too readily, only to find the grass is not really greener on the other side. Let us put our very best effort forward. There is no greater success in life than a successful marriage.

As we cross each other's paths on our journey, we will meet many people in our lifetimes. Invariably, we will find those that have similar outlooks and destinations as ourselves. As we make choices to travel with a companion, we make a silent, consensual commitment. This bond transcends all languages, all nationalities, life styles and ages. It has been in place since man himself. It is a universal joining of your energies that you willingly agree to share this moment in time with each other. You trust in them, and they in you. The power of two souls in harmony outweighs all the energy we can feel as one. It is the Tao joining all that is, in a natural unison, that we may see and feel the beauty of the whole. We are not meant to live in isolation. That disconnects us from the Tao. This is known as seeing only the small self. In seeing only the small self, we cannot be objective and are lost in our own self-interests. These selfish actions bring us sorrow and disconnect us from all of the beauty and harmony that is the Tao, the Source. When we reach out and make that human connection with another, we join the Source of all things, and leave the small self behind. There is an obvious but hidden truth here that I want to share with you.

We develop close relationships by the number of things we have in common or accept in another. The more synchronicity we share, the closer the connection.

While we acknowledge this in our lives, we seldom really apply it to understand why some relationships we have are so much deeper than others. In knowing our companions share our own views and feelings, and relate to each other with intense synchronicity, we can build some truly wonderful friendships in our lives. Friendships help us to support each other in times of weakness. They also increase the value and meaning in each experience that otherwise may have been only ordinary. They give us strength and perspective in all we do. We have found validation in our existence. I feel important and valued because this person believes in me. What a magnificent gift we have been given here! In traveling the paths of our lives with our companions, the experience has so much more meaning and value.

When we begin to find areas in our relationships where our views do not agree, know that you have found a boundary in that friendship that must be carefully negotiated. We must respect others opinions and feelings. These are walls that may or may not limit how close a relationship may become. The choice is up to you. Learn to accept that even in their mistakes, their different value systems and choices they make for themselves, that they too make these same exceptions in accepting your friendship. We must all recognize that we are created uniquely, and draw from all of our varied experiences to become who we are. The creation period of who we are is never complete. We are a changing, evolving, and remarkably beautiful entity that constantly responds to the world around us. We understand and comprehend all that we have learned to make our lives more complete and fulfilling.

Learn to understand that it is acceptable to be the bigger party in overlooking behavior that is harmless and only annoying in our friends. Here you have been given the opportunity to lead, if only quietly and by example. In time you may watch as your friends leave these behaviors behind, and truly begin to expand on their own. By using patience and being an example, you have an opportunity to gently change the world. Becoming an extraordinary person takes time and patience. Be sure to remember this as we work with others and their own unique personalities. Rest assured, no matter how great the teacher, the student will humble the master on occasion, and both may learn from each other. Observe that this is the natural cycle of the Tao working as it has forever. Never be too proud to accept humility as a student – it has much for us to learn.

In our lives we will be given very few chances to experience a relationship that has no boundaries. In these intense and deeply personal gifts that come our way, we must recognize them for what they are and learn to make the most of them while they last. Like a falling star, a rainbow, or a magnificent sunset, they will leave us all too soon with only the memory of who we were to each other to sustain us. In the relationships we share that have that special gift of deep synchronicity, let us not let the moment and value pass us by. If you have been fortunate to have experienced a miracle of indescribable oneness with another, then you understand this. If you have not, maintain your vigil, for surely within your life this chance will one day come to you. Recognize it when it comes. Make the most of it when you feel it. Love it in your heart forever when it leaves.

As we continue on in our friendships, complications will arise. We all have our differences as well as our similarities. It is our ability to overlook these faults and choices our friends make in their lives that help cement the blocks of time we share together into a lasting monument that we may both may share. Sometimes, we unfairly expect more from a relationship than it can deliver. There is an inherent wisdom that we must observe in not making more of a relationship than is really intended.

We cannot be all things to all people.

In our painting of our lives, the creation that we all are working on from our birth to our death, we apply every color that we can find to its canvas, that we may be true to ourselves and display our own character and spirit to the world in our own unique way. It is unrealistic for us to look to one individual to supply us with all of the millions of colors we will need to complete our masterpiece that is our own self-image. Recognize this in your frustrations in your relationships. Because a person does not supply you with all you need, it does not mean that they are not giving you all that they can. Appreciate what colors they have given you; the others will present themselves at the correct time, in the correct way. This is the Tao flowing naturally to you, bringing you exactly what you need when you need it. Do not be lead astray because it has not arrived when you demand it. Patience and balance, in all things we must have trust.

Our friends sometimes make unrealistic demands on us. They take advantage of the energy we exchange when they begin to see only the small self in their lives. Walk carefully here. Though we value our friendships, let us not be led in directions we do not wish to follow. Once we have traversed a distance with our companions, we long to follow them wherever they lead, even if that is a different path than is meant for us.

We all inherently "know" what path and direction we need to flow in. It is that little voice, that nudge, that returning thought and intuition that quietly whispers to us, what the correct thing for us to do is. We may push it away, but it always returns. It is the voice of the subtle energies coming through. Accept that in your life your companions may part, and walk the mountain of life alone at times. You may meet again on the trail some day, or you may not. But in either case, the correct event has occurred. Learn to accept these events. We must make thousands of connections before our journey ends. The ones that are meant to last the test of time will survive. Then there are those that seem to end all too early before we are ready, and we must look to the wisdom of the Tao, that all things are balanced and are taking the course that has been destined for them and accept it in our hearts. Recognize that in your separateness that you must continue to cross ravines, climb a solitary passage, and swim a current of pain that have all been meant for you. These challenges will be brought into our lives. There are times that we simply must just go it alone.

In taking on a Taoist life style, I have come to terms with all of these events in my heart. I help those that I can. I let go of those I cannot. Sometimes I am the student. Sometimes I am the teacher. It is truly a great man that knows how and when and to what degree a relationship is supposed to be in their lives. We tend to expect and want more from them than what they are intended to be in our existence. This can lead to a very difficult situation for both parties, and I want to caution you here.

> "- a man is rich in proportion to the number of things which he can afford to let alone."
>
> *Henry David Thoreau*

Not every flower we come across needs to be picked. By listening to the subtle energies, we will know instinctively when action is to be taken, and when we should accept events as they are, with no further interference on our part.

The small self cries out in our hearts continually. It desperately wants instant gratification. It has little patience. It can only see the shortsighted future of its own selfishness. Sometimes I look quietly at my small self, and laugh as a parent does when raising a small child. How much you have to learn! I listen instead to the Tao, which leads me to the

Source. Here I can find humbleness and truth. In looking at all of the universe and my place in it, I have risen up to the peak of the mountain, above the clouds of confusion my human nature has placed around me, and see my true destination and my purpose.

Be wise in your choices of your friends, your relationships, and your lovers. They all have value, meaning, purpose and distinction. Together you will travel the path of life while fulfilling each other's destinies. Follow your instincts to know the correct role that each one is meant to play in your life. Remember that in your search for true spirituality, giving yourself away completely with no reservation for your own interests will correctly point you toward your true destination, the compass within your heart.

The Taoist walks the earth a servant to every man. He is trusted by all, not to betray a trust. We live to be an example, and quietly influence what ever happens our way. This is known as the subtle energy that is found in all things, in many manifestations. Because man is always listening to the small self, and not the subtle energies, he is led astray. In our friendships, let us be the perspective that the world must see. If that image is not attractive, then we have become the mirror that they may see it in themselves.

"You can only live your own life honestly and let people be aware by seeing the mirror of their ugliness."

"Once a person wishes to control another, he extends his energy beyond himself to others; he loses balance."

Master Hua-Ching Ni from his fascinating book,
Entering the Tao.

Conversely, we may also show them how beautiful they are. Seldom in life do we reinforce the positive we see in each other, especially in acknowledging the depths of our friendships. It is a small mission in my life to reflect back to my friends whose relationships I treasure so deeply, that I truly value these connections and never will take them for granted. In assessing our relationships in our lives, remember to observe these few simple rules.

❖ There are thousands of ways to love and be loved. Accept whatever form comes to you, from whoever extends it. Reflect what you can back into their lives.

❖ Though I have chosen my partner in life for my own needs, it is their own needs that I must serve to sustain us both.

❖ Treat others how you wish be treated. Always.

❖ When I have done all that I can, and the small self is quiet, then I am following the correct path.

❖ As our companions wave goodbye, know in your heart that you have done all that was supposed to be done. Love it for what it was, no matter what you thought it was supposed to be. The Tao has brought the correct thing to you both. The cycle completes its path.

❖ Love your friends as yourself, forgive them as you forgive yourself, and trust in them as you trust yourself. Then you will truly honor them, as you honor yourself.

Our friendships in our lives we treasure in our hearts. They are a living affirmation that our lives are valuable and complete. They are the mirrors of ourselves, that we may measure our own self-image. If we wish to enjoy all of their rewards, we must value our relationships, that we may accurately measure ourselves against our changing world. In our new telescope that we are learning to use, there is no star that shines brighter than our relationships with those close to us. Let your light shine on them, and theirs on you, that you may both illuminate your true destinies together.

Walking With You

I smile, and the warmth of your face
    illuminates my soul.
        In each we are half,
            together we see the whole.

I give you all I have,
    and now I have it all.
        And through the hurricane of life,
            I hear your call.

The roads we've chosen,
    the storms we've weathered,
        have led us to this path
            together.

The moments we share,
    the reward I measure,
        becomes the greatest gift,
            that a man can treasure.

JR

Change

"But I can't do this, it's too hard and confusing!" I often hear this. I can tell you that I understand your feelings. Change is the single most difficult thing for a person to do. The bigger the change, the harder it is. Not a single great accomplishment has ever come from being easy. Not one. If you truly are tired of living in sadness, self-pity, and discontentment, if you want everything to suddenly make sense to you, if you really desire the very best for yourself and want to be happy not matter what life brings, you must change. We recognize the need for change, after we have experienced one of life's many storms. There is an old Chinese proverb that puts this in perspective for us.

During strong winds, a tree cannot suddenly grow deep roots.

This is so true. As we take a few rough roads in our journeys though, we discover that perhaps fate and chance may have something deeper behind them. Here we seek out ways to put down deeper roots, that the next wind in our lives not cause us so much damage. This is the first step down the path to our spiritual journey.

Your own personal spiritual growth and contentment should be your primary goals. Only from these strengths will you expand to help others. As you help others, your own intensity will grow! It is like a stone thrown into a pond. The ripples spread out to affect a wider and wider area until the whole surface is alive with motion. It all begins with the stone. You have to make the conscious decision to begin. If you are unhappy with your current life circumstances and surroundings, chances are you will not be happy in another scenario as well. So let's get started. Until now, you have lacked the tools and the instruction. I am giving you both! It all starts with *you*.

The Story of Gandhi

In studying the process of change, I found myself constantly drawn back to the story of Mahatma Gandhi. I used to tell myself, "I can not make a difference in the world, so why should I change? After all, I am only one man. What can one man hope to accomplish in his lifetime?" But after reading Gandhi's story, it gave me the courage to strive and be the very best person I could be.

Gandhi was born in 1869 in Gujarat, West India. His family lived comfortably with his father being a well-respected diplomat. His mother was a devout Hindu who helped shape her son's views on life. As was the custom, he was married at thirteen in a prearranged marriage. This was not to his liking and he later in life spoke out strongly against this custom.

At the age of nineteen Gandhi left for England to study law, leaving his wife and a young son behind. Here he found Western life difficult, but adapted with the discovery of many new friends who represented the fringe of anti-industrialist thought. Together they shared their interests in studying the major religions, as debate fueled their thoughts. He finished his degree, enrolling in the High Court of London, but left later that year to return to India.

Upon arriving back home, he discovered that his mother had passed away. He set up a law practice, but it was unsuccessful and after one year took a position in South

Africa working as a legal advisor. Here he found the gift that would awaken him.

For the first time, he found how Indians living in South Africa were severely abused under British tyranny. After being physically thrown from a passenger railcar even though he held a first class ticket, Gandhi began creating his own future. He developed the term Satyagraha (or firmness in truth) to signify his theory and practice of non-violent resistance. The dragon had been awakened.

He wrote a book detailing the Indian struggle for independence. Here he stated that both parties must resolve their differences in peace, for everyone would suffer otherwise. Only through non-violence could freedom genuinely be won. The Indians continued to be oppressed through unfair legislation, taxes and even the invalidation of all non-Christian marriages.

At the age of forty-four, he returned to India. Here he traveled widely for several years, settling disputes, teaching non-violence, and urged his people to seek their own independence. He became known as a great peacemaker within his own people where division between the Hindu and Muslim sects caused constant unrest.

After a bloody uprising against the occupying British in 1922, Gandhi was sentenced to prison for six years, charged with "sedition" by the British. Here for the first time he spoke out against the tyranny and oppression of his captors at his trial. This later was to draw him much admiration among his people. In prison he drew international attention for fasting until his release. During his stay, he spoke out widely against preferred divisions within the Hindu sect. All were equal in his eyes, and no group should be allowed favoritism. Under intense pressure and with failing health, he was released after serving three years in prison.

Taking an active role in social reform, Gandhi began to publish many articles on all manner of Indian affairs. His popularity now began to spread among many of the lower class

Indians. Conversely, he had made many enemies among the favored of his country.

At the age of sixty-one, he wrote a letter to the English Viceroy declaring the "Salt Laws" which forbade anyone except the English from mining salt to be invalid. The Indian National Congress had gained momentum by this time, a result of the nationalistic movement. The beginning of civil disobedience had begun. Thousands were arrested as they violated British law and Gandhi once again found himself in prison. To appease international opinion again, Gandhi was released to begin talks in England on the promise of Indian self-rule. After no progress was made he was sent back to India where he was once again arrested.

Upon his release, he vowed never to return to his hometown until India had won its independence. He set up a new home in the center of India with no water or electricity. Here he began to shape the future leadership for his homeland. In 1942, Gandhi made the British an ultimatum. He called for every Indian to lay down his life for India in the "Do or Die" declaration. "Quit India!" was his final demand. Britain responded by jailing the entire Indian National Congress along with Gandhi until after the end of World War Two. During his internment, one of his best friends as well as his personal secretary for many years had both passed away.

After his release at the age of seventy-four, the new government in England was genuinely sympathetic to Indian independence. As internal political struggles began to take place, Gandhi separated himself from the flag waving and credit taking. He instead proceeded to visit the rioting villages within his country, becoming a one-man wall between the Hindus and Muslims. At all costs he placed their needs before his own safety. In Calcutta, he single handedly prevented intense bloodshed that had become a focal point of an internal war. This later became known as "The miracle of Calcutta." When India announced its own independence in 1947, Gandhi was nowhere to be found. Such a humble man, he wanted no credit for all of his efforts.

In his last valiant act of courage, he would once again place himself between the violence of the Hindus who had been displaced from Pakistan and the Muslims who inhabited the capitol of Delhi. Over a million lives had been lost and over 11 million refugees had taken flight. At the age of seventy-seven, Gandhi made his last "fast until death" promise. His hand once again forced a pact between the communities. Several days later on his way to evening prayers, Gandhi was murdered by a fanatical Hindu, shot to death with a handgun; a lifetime of peace tragically ended with an angry bullet. In his last dying words he blessed his attacker, the final chapter of life now written.

The history of a nation was changed by the strength of one man, with but two arms and two legs, owning no more than the shirt on his back. Here we find that the strength of a will was stronger than all oppression combined. He was driven by his dreams. The reality he imagined came into existence with each day that he worked tirelessly to create. Despite the obstacles that confronted him, he looked continually toward the horizon, and his final destination.

In his truly selfless lifestyle, we may find the courage of change within ourselves. If one man can change the world, then surely we too hold the power of change waiting in our souls. Both Gandhi and I began our journeys in much the same way, by using the strength found in but two simple words—I can.

"You must be the change you wish to see in the world."

Mahatma Gandhi

In our search for the strength to change, we find we must become selfless. This all begins by being the best person that you can. Of everything in your life so far, is there anything more important than becoming the very best person you can be? How many of us consciously work every day toward this goal? Can you imagine how great you can become if you spent as much time at it as you do your career, your appearance or even your hobbies? Which is most important to you?

> "To be awake is to be alive. I have never yet met a man who was quite awake. How could I have looked him in the face?"
>
> *Henry David Thoreau*

It is a choice you control. Take control of your life. Life doesn't just happen! It is a natural response to who and what you project to the universe! If you project happiness and well-being, then that is what you will attract in your life. Until now you thought things just "happened" to you! There are no coincidences. The universe responds to all that you need. Be aware of these gifts when they appear. The tools you need to be happy and balanced are usually nearby. Do not look far for what is near. When you become stuck in life, stop and glance around you and ask yourself, "What am I overlooking?"

I have a friend who had a very normal life. She raised a family, supported her husband, and worked tirelessly for many years. But as problems arose, instead of effectively dealing with them, they took control of her life. She was no longer in control. Her problems began driving her. Eventually she spun out of control.

I call this the "crash course" syndrome. We lose so much control, eventually it is like being in the back seat of a moving car unable to reach the steering wheel! When we lose this much control in our lives, the big crash is inevitable. We see our friends standing by with their eyes covered, asking them "What's wrong?" Everyone could see it coming but you. By using effective change and empowering yourself to deal with life, you can regain control of the wheel. In time, you can get back into the driver's seat. Then *you* decide where you are going, and how fast and safe you will arrive. Evaluate your own current "driving" skills. Are you really in control, or do you just think you are? If you recognize the danger of the loss of control in your life, take the time to evaluate some changes that will put you back in the driver's seat. Life doesn't have to be a demolition derby; the choice to cruise on Easy Street is totally up to us.

Anything can be changed. You should not attempt too much at once. Take time to evaluate changes you have made. Getting unsolicited feedback from your changes will be your guide. Your friends and even strangers will see you differently. They will comment. Take time to write your goals down. At the end of the week, compare yourself to your model. Does it fit? If not, keep working! Write notes for yourself. Keep them on your refrigerator, your car or desk. They can be simple little phrases or even a smiley face; it doesn't matter, as long as you know what they mean. No one else needs to know. As time goes on, you will need them less and less!

Take the time every day to sit quietly and review any materials that are helping you to change. Use this book if you find it helpful. Read everything through and then *read it again.* Write down the highlights of what you find effective. In the appendix of this book is a list of favorites and suggested reading materials. Do not stop searching for your answers. Review these notes daily to help reinforce your efforts to effect your permanent changes. Remember, you have spent a lifetime using ineffective techniques. It will take patience and time to instill new and more effective tools. Be patient, you will find the need for so much study less and less as you get stronger and learn how to effectively use your new system.

I want to leave you at the end of this chapter with some taste of this alternate reality that I am taking you to. Words are difficult to convey feelings, but in your mind lay many memories. If I may borrow some of these for just a moment, I think we may be able to touch just a fragment of the Tao, and bring you understanding to the words I have written upon these pages, that we may bring them to life within you. Change can be much easier to confront if we have the urgency and the need placed clearly before us.

I was having lunch with one of my companions one day, and we were brought to the discussion of the Tao. The topic of my philosophy resurfaced, and I was asked why I did not demonstrate it more openly. This was my reply.

As a Taoist, I am humble to my very core and do not ever impress upon my fellow man any of my ideas or teachings. The change in my own life was a gift meant for me. With that gift comes the inherent power of self-controlling balance. As long as I live my life for others and do not concern myself with my own self-interests, then I always will have the Tao in my heart. If I try and shout to the world, and try to actively influence those about me, I have placed self-worth and deceit upon myself. Here the Tao cannot be felt, and it slips away. It cannot be misused, for it only can be seen and felt by pure thoughts and actions. I lead by example, and do no more. Believe me when I tell you, you will have quite a following as it is! In your calmness, openness, caring and quiet actions, these become as loud as an approaching storm. It is inevitable. People will notice! The questions will come. This is the natural cycle of the Tao. From the student you will become the teacher. From the teacher you will become the master.

After we had finished our lunch, I was asked to describe the feeling of the Tao within me.

"What was it like?" she asked.

All Taoists before me and I am sure all that will follow are perplexed to describe the Tao and how it fills them with complete solitude. In my mind I quickly began sorting through the entire rack of human emotions that I have tried on in my lifetime, and the perfect description suddenly burst through my subconscious.

"It is like being in love!" I suddenly shouted. Just like the pureness and compassion of love, it fills you up inside, and the entire world takes on a different perspective. But unlike the love we share with another, we share it with every person, every object and every event within our lives. If we continue to honor its balance, it can only grow within us and never fade. I pass it on to every human I meet, in any way I can. This not only improves their lives, but mine as well.

Reach back into time now. Remember that day when you felt so totally overwhelmed with compassion for another person. Think clearly for a moment now and draw that memory forward. Their entire existence was followed with your eye, that you not miss a single element. You wanted to take it all in, and keep it forever yours to own. This is what I feel every day, in every action I perform, observe, and experience. It is an existence of pure wonder and understanding. The result almost cannot be comprehended. While the world around me is wrapped in controversy, I am as content as an evening sky.

Human love can be so fleeting. Time fades it, self-interests break it down, and we must again begin our search for that feeling in our lives. We become reluctant to reach out though, for it has taught us pain as well. Though we long for love, we know that there is a price to be paid, and we are unwilling to afford it. The form known as the Tao knows no such limitations. It waits forever for us to touch it, hold it, and embrace it in our minds. It can never leave you, for it is woven in all events and interactions, both observed by man and those yet to be known. It is impartial as the wind and blows every minute through our souls. Only through our own proper perspective and actions can we reach it and hold it within us.

As I looked back across the table into my companion's eyes, I knew I had made a connection and had drawn her into the Tao, if only for that moment. With dedication, we may take those moments and make them last longer and longer, until all of our daily existence is filled with them. Here we no longer visit the Tao, but walk within it.

This concept is critical to reaching the final plateau of contentment. It is not reached by reading any single book. Nor is it reached in a discussion with a brilliant sage. It cannot be found in any lifestyle or person of self-interest. Even when we understand these basic principles, how do we take the next step, and when will we arrive at our new Eden? Here I can only tell you of my own experience, and what happened.

In the chapter "The Kid I Once Knew", I gave you a brief overview of how my life had ground to a halt. Now I would like to expand on how I changed myself. The key ingredient here is called *willpower*.

First, I listed all of the things in my life that I was sure of. What could I trust and value without question? I thought about my formal education. Because it had been dictated to me by a system that I no longer trusted, my knowledge had to be held with suspicion as well. Next I evaluated my career. Up to this point in my life, I had played various roles that merely amounted to being a cog in a wheel; I knew I had become part of a corporate machine, and felt somehow that those choices had made me untrue to myself. Even friends and family had to be held with some suspicion; their own views, though meaning only well and good, were also suspect to this *force* that I had only recently broken through and identified. They too had become victimized by our culture, teachings, and damaged value systems. I searched endlessly for heroes, but came up empty time and again.

A thought suddenly presented itself to me one day. What if the hero I had been searching for had been right in front of me all along? As I had begun my research into Taoism, one key point kept coming back to me; all that we need in life is readily at hand! The best solutions come from the closest and most obvious and simple sources. After thinking about this for several weeks, I had compiled a list of people that I knew had some of the most beautiful qualities that anyone could own. Though vastly different in ages, gender and roles in life, I began to connect and find a hidden bond within them that I had just begun to recognize now within myself.

My grandfather. He was a magnetic man with very riveting eyes, and always looked directly into your heart. He used many wise sayings, and taught me as a young man how to be wise, watchful and respectful. I dearly loved this man who could influence his surroundings with such genuine kindness. His funeral was a very big loss for me, and a hidden message was delivered that day that I would not read until

140

much later in my life; special people come into your life for a reason. Make the most of it while they are here, and draw from them the love and the lessons that they have brought into your life. Here was a man I could emulate, and make myself a better person. Though the years have past, the lessons have not been forgotten.

My brother, James. We have always held a bond of synchronicity that defies explanation. Here was a man who has led a very hard life, with many unfortunate difficulties. A tragic auto accident had literally shredded his body, but he fought through it all with the heart of a warrior. He never even cried for himself. Always he has worn a warm smile, and is genuinely interested in how your life is going. Though he never has had much, whatever he had was yours. His unselfish life style is a value few men can own.

My best friend, Doug. Though I was only a young boy of twelve years, I had developed a close relationship with a summer friend who I met every year. We spent much of our time running through the woods, sitting on a dock with our feet in the water, and generally learning about life one day at a time. Doug was a little different than most kids in several ways. He had a speech impediment that typically brought cruel responses from other kids. Though this seemed to isolate him, he had a heart of gold, and was a great friend. Thanks to my parents, I had been raised to accept everyone's individuality without question. My most innocent memories were shared with this boy who had such a vibrant outlook on life; every day was for having fun, and he was going out to get it!

One day Doug came down with a bad cold. Three days later he had passed away from Leukemia. It was my first experience with death, and the loss still stands vivid in my memory. Though our time together was short, I will never forget it, or the silent lessons learned that long summer without him.

My co-worker, Paul. Here was an elderly man that was a perfect gentleman. He knew many things about any topic you could bring up. But Paul never initiated a conversation. He would wait and hear what you had to say, because that was more important to him. He always spoke in a very reserved manner, and chided those among us who acted in any other way than honorable. Paul was the modern day Samurai. He lived by a code of honor. To be accepted by him, you had to live up to his moral and social values. He loved all that was right and good in this world. Every man who ever met him walked away a better person for it. I know I did.

My wife, Cindy. We fell in love on our first date. We met when we were only fourteen. We have never broken up, been separated, or even spent the night apart. To this day we must sleep every moment together while touching lightly. Always her motives in life are pure and truthful. If any man has found a greater companion, I bow to you. She has continually worked tirelessly at any task, never complains, and carries herself with humility that cannot be measured. She has given her entire self to her family, and never has asked for one thing in return. Though struck down by her health for many years, she does not allow it to control her mind. She is forever my center and my mirror. Here I have learned honor, devotion and humility. Through her eyes I have found a world that few in life will ever know. Though weakened by disease, I have the strongest warrior on Earth, right by my side. I long to spend not only the rest of this life with her, but the next as well.

After evaluating all of these people, as well as studying various characters in history, it became obvious to me that they all shared many qualities. It had never dawned on me that I had a choice in who I presented to the world every morning. If I could take the best qualities from these heroes in my life and blend them with my own true personality, could I not become a purer form of myself?

I was very busy working around the house one day, when a very intense moment caught my attention. I looked back at my wife and watched as she struggled to merely traverse a short distance from her chair to reach another room. She has periods of unbalance, and often cannot navigate even the

142

shortest distance without intense effort. She cried softly as her body abruptly met an unmoving wall, and she stumbled forward. With willpower and perseverance she pushed on to her destination.

I remember thinking to myself, "My God, what strength is denied to her body, lives quietly in her soul!" The moment was a quiet revelation, as the lessons of Lao Tzu played through my mind. Though covered in my own misery and anguish, the gift within our suffering was now mine to open. The search for my model in my quest for change was over. She was right beside me all of my life.

So it began. Baby steps upon oh so many baby steps. Whenever I began faltering though, I had only to remember her image and her impact on me to drive me forward. I had made up my mind. I would never be that old pathetic person I had become ever again. Whatever it takes, no matter what the price, I would pay it. If it took a lifetime, I would become like the image of my master who had burned her impression so vividly upon my soul. Failure was not an option. If ever the universe had sent me a more powerful lightning boltlike gift that was meant for me, it could not have been more obvious. I knew what I had to do. The question was how do I begin?

First, I had made the decision to change. That was monumental and would become the cornerstone of my new world. Second, I had to *begin reading.* This is crucial. There are so many fragments of critical knowledge scattered through out history only regarded as mere words. Humans the same as you have been through the same experiences, scattered throughout man's timeline. They have faced many of the same issues thousands of years ago! Let us not reinvent the wheel when we have not even looked about us to see what is available! When we reread these texts, these people come alive and transmit their knowledge magically through time for us to have!

I made the time in my day to study these texts, every day, rain or shine. No excuses. This was a project bigger than any I had ever known, and a challenge that I took very seriously.

I felt that I was fighting for my life. I was thirty-four years old and felt that I knew absolutely nothing about life except how to fail. I read dozens of books looking for answers, and tossed the ones that did not fit my model of who I was going to be. A friend had tipped me off in the direction of Taoism, and I began there. Here I found ideas that began to suddenly put the scattered pieces of my mind in order. Every religion and philosophy I could find was evaluated and studied. I then expanded to many other diverse texts as well. Faith and perspective can be found in many hidden materials. Once I started following my instincts, I found that they were right in front of me the whole time! I have included some of the materials that I found helpful in the appendix of this book.

It is not enough to read a text and put it down saying, "That was a good book and I really liked many of the passages!" The travels and experiences I am relating to you can be your experiences and realities too, and so much more. Time moves on, and the memories and impressions soon leave our conscience. So how do we reinforce these ideas and make them a permanent part of our lives?

I find that by rereading a book or document that is extremely motivating and taking notes as I go to be very helpful. Then, by reviewing these notes on a regular basis I can quickly regain that mental aura that the original text gave me. Think of it like this. How many of us have seen the same movie a second or third time? Every time we see it, don't we find things that we missed the first time through? You will find the same thing applies to books. I find myself rereading some books at least once a year!

Initially I read *Jonathan Livingston Seagull* three times, followed by *The Tao of Pooh* at least ten times. To this day I have read *Walden* by Henry David Thoreau over thirty times!

After reading, my mind would be calm and I could slow down my thinking enough to begin to meditate. I meditated several times a day. In this process I began ever so slowly to touch fragments of Taoism in what my friend had been describing to me. This Tao thing, it was *real!* Though I was

144

able to understand the concept, it took great effort on my part not to be discouraged with how seldom I was able to *stay* in the current of its beauty all the time. It was so wonderful— words are not perfect enough to express how incredible it felt. I actually became depressed when I could not find it, after life had beaten me down yet another time. But I kept getting back up, and answered the next bell in the ring that was my fate. I was not going to lose. By watching my wife move through life so effortlessly despite her challenges, and by reading and being patient, I slowly began to have moments of solitude and pure happiness.

Pure happiness is best described as being in a great mood for no other reason than that is how I feel inside, and is what I am projecting to the world. Sure, reality kept delivering me punches, but I kept getting back up. By allowing my mind to open and feel the Tao all around me, I allowed myself to be transparent to reality and its blows began to pass through me, unable to take me down. The more I tried to understand the Tao and hold it close to my heart, the more of these isolated moments of success I found that I could string together. Eventually it can cover your whole day, then a week, then the rest of your life. The need to constantly meditate and read gradually disappeared. The change had become permanent. There was no need to "fake it" any more; I had "made it".

No it is not easy, but nothing easy ever has any lasting value. If you really want more from life than what anyone you have ever known has, these are the steps that I have taken. In the trail of life, I began following the tracks of my fellow man. When I began to expect more from myself, there were fewer tracks to follow. I have reached a point in my journey where there are no tracks, and I am forging my own trail. By following no man, I lead myself beyond his shallow world, to a place few have ever dreamed of. It can be done. It can be done by you. Make the conscious decision to begin. It is that simple.

While daily we must struggle with life's challenges, my determination was my light to success. May you find your own light, that your own reality will one day match your dreams. The path is here within these pages. Follow it to where it leads you. The power of change holds the ability to conquer any obstacle. Contentment and success are the rewards of those that take the test of life—and pass. Those of us that adapt to adversity embrace the master that lives within each of us.

Surrender

If I have one special flower to give to you from my garden, it is one whose beauty lies hidden within. Here we find a treasure that we have previously overlooked. In our lives, we have times where we are continually bombarded with events beyond our control. We try every problem-solving tool we know, but still we cannot come to a resolution. When we find ourselves in this situation, when total hopelessness is our last resort, we have run ourselves to the end of our limits. The only emotions left are ones of despair and defeat. I share your feelings my friend. This weight becomes an immovable stone in our path and we cannot move on.

Our natural instinct is to fight, to not give in. Persistence can conquer many obstacles, but it has its limitations. So what next, do we just give up? Walking away from our problems can give us temporary relief, but it never really solves anything, does it? There is one final option I would propose to those of you who have never tried it. It has a power beyond description, and as such, I give a space to itself -

Surrender

Surrender is but one word, a very simple word. Yet it contains the power to endure beyond anything you can imagine. In surrendering yourself to an immovable obstacle, you open your heart and your soul to the universe and whisper softly, saying, "I accept what is."

In learning techniques about changing, this one can be the most difficult to master, but yet paradoxically is also the simplest to use. Our whole lives we are trained to throw our resources at a problem with wild abandon. If we are not progressing, we must work harder!

Let me tell you this now. The correct thing happens at the correct time. That is the universe and the Tao flowing just the way it always has and always will. Resistance to the natural events that happen in our lives will only bring us more pain.

Surrendering to an unsolvable situation does several things for us. It gives us time to regroup. After working unsuccessfully for so long, our frustrations cut us off from our objectivity. By taking this break and being objective, we can reassess our situation and our options. Our energies now have returned; we are more relaxed and detached.

The next key is to remove our emotions from the situation. As humans, we tend to let our emotions dictate our actions rather than our rational thoughts that are whispering quietly in the background through all the madness our minds have stirred up. By surrendering, we let those voices come through. Many solutions are found just this simple way!

It is difficult for humans to admit they have a problem that cannot be solved. It really isn't in our culture or nature. Everything must be all good, all of the time. That is what I deserve, is it not? Perhaps, but as you are learning in this book, life is a balance. By keeping all the bad stuff away, we are creating conditions for our own happiness. If a bad thing comes along and I cannot solve it, ignore it, or run away from it, then truly I have an insolvable situation that will continue to bring me sorrow and I am at its mercy. What did I do to deserve these bad things? You have done nothing at all. You are a beautiful human who has been given a universe full of possibilities and experiences to process.

By choosing to only accept some things and not all of them, you have put conditional limits on your happiness.

In surrendering, we are not giving up. There is a delicate distinction here. Giving up means refusing to deal with a problem as we align our thoughts with despair. In surrendering, we are taking an honest assessment of our situation and saying, "It is beyond my control."

Once we take that first step, several new options are open to us! Our frustrations drop behind us like a one hundred pound hiking sack that we dropped off the side of a mountain.

How far we have carried that load! By reducing our mental burden, we are able to direct those energies to several areas.

One, we can function in our daily activities again! Our jobs become more manageable. Little things become solvable again. We can rest our minds in the evening and actually learn to sleep once more.

Two, we have begun to hack off that vine of conditional happiness that we have allowed to grow through us. In telling the world I accept what I cannot control, we are learning a key element in the lesson of balance. Good things will happen. Bad things will happen. I will endure it all because I surrender myself to the universe and all that I cannot comprehend. In time, the lessons of life will be revealed, just accept that for now we don't have all the answers. Learn to endure.

Think of life as a mural the size of a football field. We start out at the base with only a small view of what is in front of us. Everyday we take a step back. In time, the picture starts coming together. By surrendering, we are acknowledging the fact that in time we shall see the big picture.

Surrendering teaches us several other valuable lessons as well. Humbleness and humility are all parts of being a complete person. By acknowledging the fact that we are not superhuman and have limitations, we have begun to learn the lesson of acceptance, a valuable tool at our disposal. Being humble means placing all things before you. By using this technique, you have begun to change the world. Because you serve life and not yourself, there is very little that will bring you unhappiness. In surrendering, we begin the understanding that there are incomprehensive events that in time will bring additional lessons in our lives. It allows us to become objective, to see a fresh perspective. In giving ourselves totally to a problem instead of fighting it, we gain new knowledge and insight that lets us function again.

Be open to all that comes your way. Everything has purpose and meaning. Accept that we cannot know it immediately, but continue to study it that we may reap the benefits it has offered. Surrendering acknowledges the fact that it is not in our control.   There is very little in this life that we actually control.   How we process our world and how we choose to react to it is all we really control.

Life is like driving a car.   We turn the wheel and it goes left.   We turn it right and it goes right.   That is the illusion of control.   If we look under the hood of life, nothing is connected to the steering wheel at all!   Life takes you where you are supposed to be.   You can spin the wheel all you want.   Hitting the brakes or standing on the gas, it doesn't really matter.   We arrive exactly where and when we are supposed to be.

Sometimes I drive my car of life while hanging out the window.   Sometimes I drive with my feet.   Sometimes I crawl in the backseat and watch it drive itself!   You see so much more in your daily travels this way!   I never have any control problems though.   By surrendering to it all, I get where I am going safely, happily, and refreshed from life itself.   I get some crazy looks, but I can assure you no one is having more fun than I am in my drive down the road of life.   Let go of that steering wheel a little, your fingers are turning white from the strain.   Life is fun—just give it a chance to drive itself.

By understanding this, we learn that surrendering is giving up that illusion of control.   So let's get where we are going naturally, with composure and contentment that there really is nothing to worry about.   Everything is exactly how it is supposed to be, every moment of every day.   Learn to surrender my friends; it will open doors for you that you never could.

In my study of myself and conversely watching others process their lives, I have some observations I want to share with you.   There is an intangible element I have alluded to in several examples within this book.   I would like to pull those together for you now that we have seen them in perspective.

My own personal history found me trying on different religions and philosophies like a teenager picking out clothes preparing for a date.   How does it look?   Does it really fit me well?   Is it fashionable?   What will people think?   But most importantly, I kept asking myself "Does it work for me?"   That question forced a new logical question forward. "What do I need it to do?"

What do we need a faith system to do for us? What are the requirements that determine the right fit for our needs? In boiling this question down to its most basic elements, I propose one word for you—*control*. Once again we find value in a simple word. A faith system or living philosophy should provide you with all of the elements that bring control back into your life. Our greatest fears and anxieties are caused by our feeling of lack of control in our lives. When it seems that all things are in chaos, and nothing is responding to our demands and actions, is this not the frustration that drives us to our faith systems? We recognize deep down that there is an element, an intangible, a shadow, a whisper or a breeze upon our lives that keeps reminding us that there are things beyond human control. Our faith allows us to appeal to those systems, in the hope of an understanding or act of divine intervention. This is a form of surrendering, is it not?

Again we must define a delicate distinction here. Because we desire to control every aspect of our lives, we have been taught to overpower, manipulate, and plot our route to this magical land where joy and contentment wait for us. But mysteriously, like squeezing a handful of sand, the tighter we grasp, the faster it slips away from us. In giving up this destructive behavior, we paradoxically receive more control in our lives due to the mere fact that we begin to follow the river of life naturally, where all of the events destined for us have patiently been waiting. When we interfere with what is a natural instinct and try to arrange our lives in patterns that are not meant for us, we are paddling away from the Tao and attempting to create our own destinations. But as we have found in our lives thus far, these destinations hold hollow rewards. What sand is given to us, we hold in our open palm. Not only do we allow it to seek its own destination, but we can also hold much more than in a tightly clenched fist. Here we see how the power of Wu Wei provides more for us effortlessly.

151

In learning to surrender our delusional veil of control, we begin to put the first brick in place in learning to be humble. In looking at life from the perspective of not what we need, but what can we *give*, we have turned the tables on our attitude. In return, paradoxically all we need is returned in perfect harmony. Balance in perfect harmony, just what we have been seeking.

> "Surrender yourself to humility, then you can be trusted to care for all things.
> Love the world as yourself and you can truly care for all things."
>
> *Lao Tzu*

We follow these paths in response to our own basic human requirement to have some form of control in our lives. "If I'm not driving this car, than who is?" becomes our first thought. It is really important for people to feel that they have some control in their lives. In my own search for answers, I know it was my ultimate goal. I felt like a survivor on the ocean. My life raft was taking on water and I was at the will of the storm of life. So it began, my search for control.

In realizing finally that how I reacted to all of my problems was really all the control I had in life, it was such an amazing relief! I wasn't holding the world up on my shoulders like Atlas after all! Set your world down my friends, it will survive just fine. In knowing that certain events are predestined for us, and all we can do is take the message and grasp its meaning, there is no requirement for us to be constantly saving the world. I didn't sign up for this miraculous feat, and neither did you.

I want you to rest peacefully tonight. Before turning out the light and closing the book on another day in your life, walk to your closet and mentally see your Superman costume hanging there, retired now forever. You won't need it any longer. The power you have given yourself in surrendering has far exceeded all you ever could be as Superman. Sweet dreams.

The Painter

It is important to view life as a painter views their palette. There are many choices and many colors to make. Our color wheel is made up of all the experiences we have had. It is important to see that our destiny has already added colors to our canvas! It is up to us to create what we can with what we are given. Sometimes we are given bright and cheerful colors. (The "good" things.) These are easy to make a beautiful masterpiece to enjoy. But what do we do with the blacks and the grays? (The "bad" things.) It seems like no matter how much color we add to the picture, they just become absorbed into the collage and we give in. At this point the darkness is all you will see. It is all that you can imagine in your mind's eye.

Be objective and continue to paint with what you have. I have found that most of us have put our brushes down, our work complete.

"This is who I am!" is the common response. Then I always ask them the same question.

"But is this who you want to be?" I show them my painting, and quietly after much contemplation, they pick up their brushes and pick up where they left off.

See an image that is where you want to be. Continue to work toward your goals. There is no time limit and no judge. It must become what *you* see in your heart. Beauty is in the eye of the beholder. Paint to please your own eye, not what you think others would prefer. For the creation that you were destined to be revealed, we must trust that each of us holds the wings of an angel within our souls. In our paintings, we are bringing that to the surface for the whole world to see! The possibilities are endless. Choose to make the best of things. With patience, beautiful pictures will form as you adapt and learn to use what you have found. In studying the Tao, we learn that we can experience and use all of the colors in our lives. They all have purpose and meaning, sometimes far beyond our own understanding. Learn to endure. It is important not to give up. In experiencing both pain and pleasure, we learn a spectrum of lessons from both. Both are equally important. In living our lives with perspective, there becomes less distinction between the two. In each pleasure there can be found sorrow, and in each sadness lay a hidden joy. They have for eternity coexisted within each other, thus the equation is balanced at all times.

In a single word, there is a complete picture here I am trying to paint for you—*balance*. It cannot be overstated how important this word is. Behind every light, a shadow stands. In our own lives, we have many images that make up who we are. When we are sad, we are a blue gray color, hidden in the darkness. When we are happy we are the color of the sun, illuminating others lives with our light. The choice of who we wish to display to the world is totally up to us. In the person you are creating, you are drawing from many experiences both good and bad. Understand that in the cycle of life, you must choose to paint the best you can with what resources you have. Show the world what you can do. We all look at each other's paintings every day. Create your masterpiece for all to see, show it to the world. It is really all the control that we really have in this life.

Everyone knows what a color wheel is. We all have seen a canvas and have held a paintbrush. Everything I am telling you can also be found in other various forms. It is my artistic impression of the picture I have prepared for you that is the difference here. In understanding the Tao, I am placing all of the colors I have collected into the most intriguing picture that I know how to create. It may never be completed. It, like myself is a work in progress. In these pages I give to you all that I know. My painting is yours forever, a gift from me to you. In time, maybe you can take it farther than I ever dreamed. The endless beauty of the Tao reaches out across time, distance, and an entire universe to reach you. Pick up your brush, become the master. What a world we would have to look at if we all became as beautiful as we could be. We can all be so much more. Uncover the painting that lies in your color wheel, it has been waiting quietly for you.

Meditation

It became obvious to me from the very beginning of my search for a deeper understanding of life, that I would need many tools to rebuild myself. The image I had settled on in my mind of who I was going to be was one of an immense palace; quite a vast comparison to the simple shack I imagined myself to be starting with!

It was clear that I needed some way to close the gap between my body and my mind. While we perform our daily activities, these two are not always in synchronicity with each other. As time goes by we loose the ability to really connect with our inner self, and we soon become dysfunctional. Seeking all the possible solutions, I began reading publications on how to perform meditation. It was rather awkward to begin, but I knew it was something that I wanted to try. The benefits that I had read about from so many sources must certainly hold some value.

The basic elements are very simple, and can be modified to suit your own tastes. Begin with a quiet place where you are comfortable. This can be indoors or outside. Close your eyes and try and relax. Do not fall asleep though! The idea here is to quiet your mind. Stop all thoughts from entering; yes, everything! It will take some practice, but in time the world will drift off into the distance, and you will find a level of quiet that you never knew existed. In order to find this quietness, it is necessary to focus sometimes on an imaginary object or scene. Some like to picture a beautiful sunset on a quiet shoreline. The only sounds are the waves lapping on the sand. Others like to focus on an object within their mind, perhaps a favorite painting that has captured their imagination. Many techniques use a simple phrase or word repeated over and over. After several attempts, I began to find that the sessions were totally mine to own. I was the director, the actor, and the audience as well. The possibilities were endless.

I eventually developed a very powerful image that immediately set my mind at peace. I would picture a moonlit ocean, clear and bright. The waves would quietly call out in their endless journey. The moon was full and huge, the ocean sparkling with its gentle beams. As I pictured myself standing on the edge of a cliff watching this night scene, a huge dragon would appear, and wait for me to climb aboard! In his spine, there was a natural seat formed by a broken spinal bone that allowed me to stay in place. Once onboard, he would leap to the air! We would fly just over the water, watching the sea below, the moon casting our shadow off of the water as it raced just below us. The sound of his wings beating I could hear, and his heartbeat and the warmth of his energy I could feel through his scales. As we flew, his color would change in many rainbow hues, each scale taking on a different color as the light danced off of it. The smell of the ocean tingled my nose as the constant flow of passing air blew my hair in the wind. I would watch as miles of shoreline disappeared, only to lead us to a small island where he would set me down, and silently fly away. If I needed more time to calm my mind, we flew longer. If I was relaxed, the island was not very far away. There I would turn on my senses to feel the world in a way that I never had known before. When I would open my eyes, I would emerge very relaxed and at peace, with the connection of the experience still vivid in my mind. It would help me center myself, and I was ready to take on the world for yet one more day.

Another method found me resting outside, again in a relaxed position. Picture yourself from a third person view, a camera above you, as you vision yourself resting below. The camera has become airborne, and begins drifting upwards. Continue to view yourself sitting in the same position, but now the camera is expanding the view, taking in more of the countryside around you. Notice the landmarks and their relative positions from where you are still seated. Watch yourself still while the camera now moves past the clouds, the atmosphere, and out into space. Your image is but a dot below now. See the satellites, the comets and the moon as the camera continues to recede from you. Now it has traveled into the Horse Head Nebula, stars are being formed as black holes are picking up all the cosmic debris. Still you see that small spec back on earth.

Now begin picturing the return journey of the camera and the view of yourself resting on the ground as it passes once more through space, the clouds, and the atmosphere. I would hear an airplane in the distance and suddenly it would appear in my camera's view! Now it is just above you once again, and you have returned from your little journey. You open your eyes feeling calm and refreshed. This technique allows me to feel humbled by seeing my place in the world while at the same time practicing the Taoist vision of always seeing the "Bigger Picture" of all that is happening around me. It really can be a most satisfying experience, one like no other you have felt before. It all begins by giving yourself the power to go places and do things that you have never attempted. Do not feel embarrassed or shy about these techniques; only you have to know. Once you experience the power inside yourself that they have given you, it will become a practice you seek out and look forward to eagerly.

After you have practiced it a few times, you will find that it only takes a few minutes out of your busy day to reenergize yourself. Take the time to turn the world off. Just reach out and turn the button to off, for just a few minutes a day. I cannot describe how different you will feel! In searching for true peace in our lives, we need more than just concepts and ideology. By bringing your body into the Tao it brings a deeper understanding of the great mystery. Some call it "being in the moment." We tend to ignore these ideas because they are so "nontraditional." Remember, traditional ideas have not brought you the insight you have been seeking. Be open to change. Live a little. Think of it as a refreshing bath for your mind. Here is an interesting story to demonstrate.

While recovering from surgery due to cancer, I awoke three days later to find many tubes and incisions in my body. The pain was very intense. They had been giving me morphine in my IV injection pump for three days, which was keeping me unconscious and nauseated. When my wife pointed this out to me in one of my more lucid moments, I quit pushing the button that was supposed to be giving me pain relief. In a matter of hours I felt so much better!

I had some very good caregivers, and also some that were less than diligent. Again we see the balance of the Tao here. One of my nurses came in to take my vitals and check my bandages. "I have a different pain medication for you," she called out as she entered the room with a large syringe. I had been meditating and she was amazed to find me sitting up and smiling. I politely told her that I would not need any pain medication. I had adjusted my body to accept my current condition, and I was feeling much better. Well my, my, that was certainly not the traditional response she was used to hearing! But I was not the traditional patient. She thought I was delusional. The staff seemed very surprised that I was rejecting their medications. I repeatedly assured them that for me, this was the best course, and that I would let them know if I changed my mind. Reluctantly they agreed. I just kept smiling and laughing with them. It was quite an entertaining day for me. New staff I had not seen before would "pop in" for a visit. I would greet them cheerfully, and insist on talking about them, and not myself. I continually steered the conversation back to their lives. My situation was of no concern to me. I had faith that in the Tao, all would work out for the best and that I accepted any outcome. When my visitors left, they never knew what had hit them. By the third day after discontinuing the medication, I had a regular audience that just kept "popping in" to check in on me. It was so much fun!

With practice we can actually reduce or sometimes even disconnect the wiring that gives us pain in our body. The greater the pain, the less likely we will be to totally overcome it, but with practice we can make it more tolerable. In the summer, I do not sweat. I reach inside myself and turn it off. In the winter, I wear very light clothing, choosing to be less encumbered while being totally comfortable. I watch for signs of danger, but none appear.

After I finished my chemotherapy I was given the option of radiation treatment. With the immense size of my original tumor, and the added success rate of the combined treatment, I agreed to receive radiation every day for six weeks. I had been advised of the risks and agreed to begin immediately. While I strongly advocate the power of the mind, we must also learn when we should rely on all the resources available to us. With the advances in medicine in cancer treatment, and the powerful tools at the medical world's disposal, it was an easy decision to let them do what they knew best, and I would do what I knew best. Together I figured I could not lose. Again we see the power of Wu Wei; without effort, I would let the medicine and my own mental strength cure myself. After the treatments were over, I began the long recovery process. It indeed was to be a very long road. I felt like I had aged thirty years. This had become the test of a lifetime. Now it had become my turn to see what I could do with what the doctors had salvaged.

Shortly after my treatments were over, I began having many strange and intense burning sensations in my back, shoulders and arms. They became more frequent and intense, and began to involve many other muscle groups, giving me intense pain that I could not overcome. I could not sleep, concentrate on my work, or turn this off in my mind. "Another challenge to overcome," I remember thinking, as I called my oncologist yet one more time. After more exhaustive testing and retesting, the good news was that I was still in remission. The bad news we found was possible spinal damage caused by the radiation that was needed to save my life. A trade we all surely would have made. After several medication changes, we found a powerful anti-seizure drug that disconnected the neural pathways without using pain medication. But the side effects were very discomforting. I was told that I might have to take this medication for the rest of my life. I found this very distressing and unacceptable. Several times I discontinued my meds, but always with the same results—intense and relentless pain.

It was obvious the medical world had taken me as far as they could, and I was grateful for that. I had been working on a new meditation visualization technique for several years, and it was time to put the throttle down and see what I could do.

Ideally, I would sit down on the ground outside. Legs crossed, with my forearms resting lightly on my knees, I would close my eyes. I would picture in my mind all of the trees in the world, the plants, the streams and the oceans. Here they shared one common bond that all of life as we know it passes through—the ground below me. I would picture this energy as a blue light of flashing intensity, coming from every element of nature from thousands of miles around. As it came nearer to me, racing underground, it would grow in intensity and life giving power. For just one moment in time I would ask that all of my fellow companions of nature share with me just a fraction what they could. Combined, I would take it all in and let it heal me. As it entered my feet, I could imagine it entering my blood, flowing upward, seeking out any renegade cells and healing them. As it approached my torso, I would picture my organs, one by one turning a healthy blue. I imagined it rising through my lungs, extending into my heart and finally my brain. By now the exercise had my senses heightened, and I would be in meditation overdrive. As the energy completed its cleansing, it would leap out of my fingertips and return to the sky, a lightning bolt exiting my body. The sessions became very powerful, and when I opened my eyes, I was not quite sure that indeed I had not been struck by lightning! It was so refreshing I decided I would keep the exercises up, just to help with my personal tranquility. Though the pain continued to wrack my body, I did not give up.

Then something strange happened. Between doses of medication, I could always tell when the pills were wearing off. I would have breakthrough pain for several hours until the next dose kicked in. One day though, no pain came to haunt me! I watched this closely for several days, not wanting to be too optimistic. But after three days, not even a twinge. Without permission from my doctor, I quietly reduced my dosage. Still no pain! I was ecstatic! After two weeks, I stopped the drug completely. Not one moment of pain, ever. My body had healed itself. There is no doubt in my mind that the intense meditation sessions were the real story behind the pains departure. My doctors smile as they shake their heads at me. "If anyone could do it Joe, I'm sure it would be you!"

The power of the mind is so amazingly incredible, it must be seen to be believed. Meditation gives us that control. As you first begin your adventures in this arena, the immediate rewards it provides you will make you continually return for another session. This is fine. We need time to heal from all of the damage that has occurred in our life, and a new-found release is just the cure for you. In time, once you adopt proper attitudes and behavior, you will find that you need it less and less. Because nothing disturbs your harmony, you find little need to "clean" your mind. This is a sign that you are on the right path. Meditation is just another tool for you to improve yourself, to make you stronger.

Use all of the tools I am describing for you. The intricate masterpiece that you are becoming will reflect the craftsmanship you are developing. In understanding the Tao, we learn to take it all in. Meditation will bring you new understanding in your journey, a new path uncovered. Follow it to where it leads you, for the beauty of the Tao in its infinite cycle, reveals once more that there is so much more to life than what we have known up to now! Close your eyes and tell the universe, "I accept it all."

Being Humble

When I was young, I used to wonder about people that were not kind; lying, treachery, self-serving, you have met them too. They are vast in number. No matter what they have, there is never enough; whatever it takes to get ahead. Worse yet, they are not all strangers. They are friends, relatives, teachers, employers, and civic leaders. What kind of world do I live in? These thoughts distressed me very much. I felt isolated. As the years passed, I was sure I was a foreign visitor to this planet. Surely I am no part of this mess! I used to joke about the mother ship coming any day to pick me up and take me home. I spent many hours sitting on a hill overlooking a valley just imaging what it would be like. I wanted to find my own kind, my people, people like myself. I could not rationalize their existence and my place in this whole program known as life. This world would be a great place if only *people* weren't in the way!

As I came to understand the Tao, my confusion melted away. My frustration was replaced by compassion. What I discovered was that my people were actually right here all along. It was just that they had never evolved and grown as complete humans. My frustration was in watching them wander and suffer as they continued to disrupt the natural harmony and rhythms that I experienced with no effort. This hidden gift I had been given was also a double-edged sword; though I had been given a key to one world, it also had been preventing me from accepting the other. In time, I also was able to uncover a few of life's natural, pure and amazing angels. The balance of the Tao was revealing all things to me in time. Ever so slowly my objectivity was being rewarded.

It was here that I discovered the secret of Taoism. I didn't need to *learn* anything to become a better person or be happier in my life. What I had to do was *unlearn* what I already had accepted as conditions for my happiness. One at a time, I removed the desires and requirements that I had acquired in living in a traditional world. When the work was complete, I found that I had come full circle in my training in life. As a child I had been innocent and happy. As a boy I had discovered desire and needs. As a man, I had sought the tools to build this machine that would fulfill my life. When I threw the switch though, it exploded into fragments, and here I found suffering. After giving up on wanting for myself, I had unlearned need. After giving up on knowledge, I had learned compassion. The man I had been seeking and trying to rebuild did not need to be created at all. He had been living inside me my whole life. What a miracle it was to meet him! Once the secret to the Uncarved Block had shown itself, I could only live the rest of my life as a humble Taoist. Here I found that there is no purer form of a man. In the process of unlearning, all of the doors of wisdom were now open for me.

With the gift of true wisdom, my perspectives began to change rapidly. There was no need to hope for a different existence; it was time to get to work and bring these wanderers a new view of life! I had taken the first lesson in learning to expand myself, beyond myself, for pure and selfless reason. These people I used to look at with indifference, I now loved! How can this be? Nothing had changed. But yet, something did change. My perspective was transformed. I no longer felt coldness, but sorrow and compassion. How terrible it must be to live inside that person! They are in constant agony and react negatively to everything in order to have some form of self-esteem. Their actions are purely self-centered. It is the only form of happiness they know. How very tragic. I now saw the world through new eyes. Lashing out at these people merely added to the cruelty they were suffering. What they really needed was help.

With a new understanding of the world, I followed the principles of the Tao. All are treated as equals. Everyone gets a smile and a warm "Hello!" I open doors for every human I can beat to the handle. "Thank you so very much!" follows every action of anyone performing their daily duties. I shovel their snow without asking. I trade places in line at the grocery store. I wait patiently for pedestrians and hold traffic for them to cross. I jump to pick up their falling articles. Only by example can we lead. In time, they will notice you. They have questions too. When they see how pleasant you are, it starts their own introspection. Questions will lead to actions. Perhaps, just maybe, you will plant a seed. At the very least you have brightened their day for that one brief moment. In turn they may do the same for another. The whirlpool in action, that we may touch everyone in some way.

It is being humble that exemplifies the concept of the Tao. Through humility we learn to serve. We serve the world now. All your actions are focused on maintaining this calm and peaceful fulfilling spirit that you now carry in your heart. It was always there. You just had to uncover it. There was nothing missing in you when you were born. You were complete, with no defects in your soul. In growing spiritually, we are merely uncovering the light that you are, one piece at a time. It has been your life experiences that have led you to thinking you are not perfect. If we let a lifetime of bad behavior and self-indulgent actions bury our souls, our light, then truly we are lost. I urge you to look into yourself. If you truly wish the power of happiness to be your every thought, your every word, your every act, discover yourself! You are not changing; you are merely recognizing your true self by washing your face, the old dirt rinsed away and seeing your own true self for the very first time in the mirror! We are all angels, earning our wings one day at a time.

When you know the true feeling that is the Tao, it is an addiction to follow it in every action of your life. You can't wait to get up in the morning! Every day it grows stronger inside you. No wonder you have compassion for the masses now. It all begins by being humble.

I would like to share with you my favorite passage from the Tao Te Ching. In three short phrases, it encompasses all that embodies the spirit of Taoism.

The sage follows all things, thus he leads from behind.
In his detachment, he is one with all things.

Having no desires, he becomes selfless, content and fulfilled.

From chapter 7 of the Tao Te Ching

I have read these lines a thousand times, and I am still in awe at the wisdom they encompass. In times of stress, I find myself repeating these in my mind.

In the first line, we are reminded of our duty to be humble. Only by being humble and placing all things before our own needs can we understand all that is the Tao. By not being concerned with all of the trivialities of life, we are not confused or led astray. Our focus is on the Tao, not on ourselves. By proper action, we can appreciate all that is. In knowing our place, we may also know balance. Such a miracle to behold!

The second line encompasses the essence of the great Tao—*detachment.* By removing yourself from the freight train that has become our lives, you now join the Tao in unison with the universe and all that it is. There you will find understanding. Serenity flows through you in all your actions.

Have you ever walked in an area that you previously had driven by only in a car many times? Perhaps it was a farm road or just a street on your way to work. Suddenly you notice so many things you never saw before! This is the lesson of detachment. By slowing your life down and taking a deep breath, you will find many new things to explore!

By stepping off of the "train," the bonds of modern man slip away. You are free to be at peace. Watch it pull away while you quietly take in the world within your world. By taking time to watch and feel all that is going on around you, you will reach a deeper understanding of the Tao. Once you experience the miracle of the world within your world, you will want to become more than just a visitor. Detachment helps us to focus and keep our perspective. It is perhaps the greatest lesson of the Tao. Remember this.

The last line is the model for all Taoist actions. Moving in unison with the Tao fulfills our lives. In transmitting our energy to those around us, we receive all the power and light of our actions reflected back into our lives with abundance.

We use this power to improve ourselves, to be stronger and happier. In the silence of our selflessness, we listen to the echo of the Tao, passing back to us. In an unending drama of birth, death, and all of the experiences both in-between and after we pass beyond this existence, the Tao continues to bring all to fruition. Stars coming to life, solar systems being formed and entire galaxies revolving in harmony; the Tao is everywhere and is everything. In an unending constant motion and in perfect balance, it silently touches every aspect of life with a synchronicity we have just now in our lives begun to understand. Here the sage's fulfillment is now overflowing. How complete her life now is!

By learning the lesson of humility, we come to see how our own needs keep us from joining this universal dance. How wonderful to know its existence and where we lie in the great mural of the universe! In this respect, we can see just how modest our lives truly are. Remember this the next time you are feeling distressed, disconnected, and disillusioned with your life. Keep the "Big Picture" in your mind at all times. It is a Taoist vigil to constantly be monitoring her own actions that they not separate her from the enticing solitude, which calls now from every corner of the Heavens. Once you arrive, you will remember all that has opened this door for you.

In our own introspection, we find that in each strength there is a hidden weakness, and within each weakness, we may find a hidden strength. Humility lets us discern the delicate distinctions of which appears as genuine, and which is the illusion. This is the secret to balance.

Ultimate goodness is like water,
Which nourishes all things with no expectations,
It is content to flow and seeks even the low places.
Thus it follows the Tao.

In dwelling, live close to the ground.
In thought, remain pure.
In disagreement, be humble and forgiving.

In ruling, use wisdom, not force.
In labor, complete the task.

With humility comes understanding.
With understanding comes great wisdom.
With great wisdom comes great respect.

From chapter 8 of the Tao Te Ching

Humbleness is the key that the great sages use to find the Tao, the hidden jewel within your heart. It takes a great and pure heart to keep it safe for the world to see. Only you have the strength to discover that person. Listen carefully. She calls quietly from inside you.

Desire

Be aware of your desires. Desires often lead to disappointment. When desires are followed, they seldom meet your expectations. New desires are followed, and again we are led down the difficult path. A desire is merely a prerequisite for your own happiness. It also is a self-imposed limitation on your contentment. When you feel strong desire, remember to ask yourself, "Does this serve others, or just myself?" If the answer is you, then you know you must control it. This includes your material possessions that you own and those that you would wish to own. The more importance you place on them, the more control they have over you. Ask yourself, "How much do I need to be happy?" In time, this list will be very short indeed! By reducing your requirements for possessions, you will enjoy a greater freedom from them.

> "I am want to think that men are not so much the keeper of herds as herds are the keepers of men, the former so much freer."
>
> *Henry David Thoreau*

Here is another piece of knowledge I have found for you. *Life is not about you.* Read that line again. That's right! The world does not revolve around you! In Taoism, we have learned that it is the function of the whole, not the part, which brings the union of all that is to its fruition. We are part of the entire cosmic system that is known and unknown to man. If we think and act as an individual with only our own interests in mind, we will lose touch with the Tao. That is the current state of mankind.

Our modern society has shown us this model of self-indulgence and a personal interest system that is currently the rage the world over. Do you accept it? I do not. Neither should you. Your own happiness is brought by serving the world. True peace in your heart lays waiting for you patiently in a place hidden closer than you can imagine. This door cannot be opened by any other key than one that a truly selfless life can forge. I am talking about right here and now! Not in some afterlife land that may or may not exist. There are no wings that will carry you higher to the Heaven you seek.

"The most exquisite paradox...as soon as you give it all up, you can have it all... As long as you want power, you can't have it. The minute you don't want power, you'll have more than you ever dreamed possible."

Ram Dass

Most of our own unhappiness and discontentments are caused by goals and desires we believe we cannot achieve. Some we know we cannot reach. That doesn't seem to stop us from agonizing over them. Most of the time we don't even realize that these are the real source of our problems. Think about it. When you are sad, or something is bothering you, what is the actual source? When we repeatedly have the same issue, it is time to evaluate our values and desires. I can guarantee you that after a thorough examination, it is usually a desire that is bringing you sorrow. This desire may be completely out of your control, an act of fate that we must carry.

Tragedy knows no limits—a broken marriage, an incurable illness, the death of a child. All these crosses we have been given to bear. Our human desire is to go back in time, to have it all back. It is important to take time to grieve. We are emotional creatures. It is a tool that helps us to process our lives. But like all tools, it has its limits. If we keep a desire to relive the past, to have things "the way they used to be," we are now nailed to the cross that we carry. It can never be put down.

Put your sorrows to rest my friends, life goes on. The sun will rise again tomorrow. It rises to greet you, to show you that in each day, a chance to begin anew is born. Marvel at its beauty. The Tao gives birth to the ten thousand things. It is an endless cycle that has been in place for eternity, and will continue on far beyond our own lifetimes. Understand that the patterns you see and feel are all part of this existence. Learn to give yourself to it. There is contentment and peace in understanding the Tao. When we practice this genuinely in our hearts, we leave the weight of our past, our crosses, behind us that we may continue on into the future.

In learning the Tao, we are taught to release our needs. In time, with practice, letting things go becomes a true path in our climb. It is not easy. It may be the hardest thing you will ever do.

In its stillness, the Tao appears transparent and indifferent.
Yet like nature,
It flows through all things,
Thus all things are complete.

If leaders of men understood this,
The ten thousand things would rise and fall,
Naturally within the people.
They would return to their humble selves,
And be at one with the universe once again.

Free from desire,
They would cease to struggle, thus attaining peace,
By appearing not to do anything at all.

From chapter 37 of the Tao Te Ching

Here Lao Tzu tells us by reducing our desires, we find ourselves. By letting go, we lose the bottomless void that we try endlessly our whole lives to fill. It cannot be done. It is good to have goals. We need to constantly challenge ourselves. To be the best we can, we need to explore the limits of our talents. When we reach certain levels, it can be a great milestone, a cause to celebrate. Lao Tzu teaches us that when we find great resistance, we may not be following the signs of the Tao. We are paddling against the current. Learning when to let things go is the great secret of the sage. Like the sage, we should relax and know when to quietly follow the river. It will lead you to where you are supposed to be. Let your desire go, and watch as it is washed away in the current. Close your eyes and be content with where the Tao takes you.

Remember, wherever you are, is the right place to be. Learn to just let life happen. Once free of your desires, the butterfly has now emerged, a gift for the world to see, in the freedom it has given itself.

Joseph Roggenbeck

The Boy that Would Fly

There was once a boy who longed to fly. He would watch for hours as the young hawks glided above him, swooping and diving. More than anything else, he would like to be a hawk instead of a boy. Instead of studying his schoolwork, he would instead go to the ridge of the valley where the birds daily gathered.

One day the boy arrived to find an old man sitting quietly in the spot where the boy had come to watch. The boy bowed politely in respect toward the old man.

"Are they not the most beautiful creatures?" whispered the boy.

"Yes, they are," replied the old man. "They earn their place under heaven every day."

The boy was puzzled by this comment. They were carefree, with the entire sky to roam! Surely they were the most fortunate creatures of the earth!

"I long one day to fly like they do" said the boy. "There is nothing that I would desire more than that." The old man eyed the boy curiously for a moment.

"So that is your dream, to fly as a hawk?" asked the old man, as he continued to follow the birds in flight.

"Certainly!" cried the boy. "I would keep one if I could, that I may capture his spirit and be one myself!" The old man smiled gently at this and asked the boy if he was sure this was what he really wanted. Unwavering in his desire, the boy quickly nodded, "Oh yes!"

At this the old man picked up a blanket that had been wrapped beside him. Inside was a young hawk, trapped inside a small cage. The old man wordlessly handed it over to the boy who was beyond words.

"I will never forget the gift you have given me!" he cried. At this the old man only smiled and followed the birds in the air once again.

The boy returned home with his new prize. He placed the cage beside his bed and watched the bird carefully for hours. After a time, he drifted off to sleep and began to dream. In his dream, the hawk spoke to him! Rather than live his life in a cage, he would exchange places with the boy. The boy was ecstatic as he agreed to trade places. Slowly the boy opened the cage. In that instant, he had wings! He had feathers! He was strong and full of life! He leapt to the air, and headed out into the sky! Here he swooped, dove, and climbed ever so gracefully as the wind lifted him ever higher. For hours he danced about, trying his new-found freedom. It was all he ever imagined it to be.

As he looked down, he began to notice that the scenery had changed. He was not quite sure where his home had been. As he continued on, he became very concerned that in his flying, he had forgotten to watch where he had been going. Traveling as a hawk, he had covered ground faster than he could imagine. Eventually he had become very tired. He must rest before he could continue. As he approached the ground, he noticed that there were only miles of open fields. As he landed, his wings had become as heavy as logs from exhaustion. It had never occurred to him it took so much work to fly!

No sooner had he landed, than a hungry leopard had sprung upon him, catching the hawk by surprise. He once again took flight, and narrowly escaped with his life. He was very hungry as he flew on, exhausted and frightened. This was becoming harder than he had expected. As he approached a shoreline, he found still no refuge, only cliffs and more rock. Beyond the vast waters below lay a land, full of trees.

"If I can just make it there, I will be fine" he thought. As he headed out over the sea, he began to tire quickly. The winds were strong here, and he found that he could fly no more. He had reached the end of his endurance. With only open water below him, he screeched with joy as a small fishing boat appeared on the horizon. As he struggled with his last ounce of strength, he tried to land on one of the ship's masts, but found his strength had left him, as he tumbled onto the deck instead. The relief to his exhausted body overcame the pain of the fall. "I made it!" he thought to himself. Suddenly though, he found himself in darkness as he was thrust into a sack by one of the crew of the ship. Desperately he beat his wings, but he was trapped inside. Never in his life had he felt so despondent and hopeless. All he ever had wanted to do was fly! For days he was unable to see even light. Surely he would die here. What a foolish boy he had been. There was so much more to flying and being a hawk that he had never thought of.

Outside the bag he began to hear voices. He found himself pulled from the bag and thrust into a cage. As he squinted in the daylight, he found that he had been taken to a market to be auctioned.

"Oh no!" he cried. "I do not want to spend my life in a cage! I have become a hawk only to be denied my freedom!" He heard the sound of a familiar voice. Who was this? It was so familiar! Suddenly the boy he had once been appeared in front of him. Eying the cage curiously, the boy spoke to him.

"So, we meet again young master. What was once free is caged, and what was once caged is now free. What have you learned about being a hawk?"

The hawk lowered his head in despair. With gifts nature gives us, also comes responsibility and burdens well hidden. No creature leads a life without a care. If only he could be a boy again, he would never want for anything ever again. Hearing his thoughts, the boy made an offer.

"If we exchange places yet again, would you free me that I may return to my home?"

"Yes!" cried the hawk, beating his wings against the cage. "I promise!" At this the boy suddenly woke from his dream.

"I am myself once more!" he called out as he touched his skin and flexed his arms. How miserable he had been, and now he was home safe in bed! His home looked more beautiful than it ever had before. He looked over at the young hawk sitting in the cage the old man had given him. He ran to the cage and released the hawk to the air. In but a simple dream, a lesson had set them both free. He would indeed never forget the gift the old man had given him.

In searching for his desire, the boy was led down the path of deception. In seeking to attain things for himself, he was led to his own misery. He had found that with every desire come additional responsibilities and obligations as well. If we take the time to find out what we really want in life, you will find the answer is to be at peace with yourself. The tools for that peace lay within you. In feeding your desires, you too may one day know the path of the young boy who would fly.

"A child cries because his needs are unfulfilled. A man cries because he still thinks as a child."

JR

Concepts

In the process of trying to reach a new understanding of our lives, it is necessary for us to think outside the guidelines we have traditionally used. The mind is an incredible tool. It can shape, paint, forge and melt ideas, words, and colors into worlds and images we have never conceived. What is sometimes required though, for us to reach these new plateaus, is a catalyst of originality. Something has to walk into our senses, and rock our imaginations into a new channel that on its own would not have been achievable. Once we break out into these new arenas of thought, the gates are open! New thoughts and ideas may now begin flooding through our minds, all of our own creation.

In this chapter I have attempted to do just that for you. In the telescopes we have viewed life from thus far, I want to suddenly redirect your attention to a view, which is quite different from all that you have known. In this corner of my mind, I want to expose you to some interesting concepts that hopefully will lead you down some new paths of thought. Though simple in structure, do not underestimate their potential value in expanding your perspective. It is only the open mind, which can solve the unsolvable, reach the unreachable, and thus achieve the unachievable.

The Cart

Picture your life as a horse drawn cart. We each get hooked up to this cart at an early age. As the burdens of life pile up, they become stones thrown into our cart. Some of us are very good at plodding. We maintain our course and just keep on pulling the load. Eventually the load becomes staggering after years of our unsolved troubles and problems have piled up within it. But all we know how to do is to keep on pulling the load. We don't dare stop! A cart this heavy could never get going again once it came to rest!

But stop it eventually will. Pulling these loads for so long, even the strongest horse will succumb to exhaustion. What now? All that we have learned is how to pull the cart; it is of no use to us now. Sometimes we get a helping hand. This can be an outsider who assists you the only way they know how. But pulling the load again does not solve your problems! With the weight of what you bare, it will soon become immovable again.

This is where you must make a decision. Do I stop here, and live in my sorrows, or find a way to unload some of these stones? Starting with even one stone will help. The desire to change will drive your ambition to find ways to empty your cart. In understanding the Tao, we learn to accept what is. By understanding that life is a balance, we begin to see the truth in all of our past experiences. Instead of stones, we can turn them into useful tools to help make us stronger. Remove the stones one by one, and build a bridge of stone to cross that gorge that is holding you back.

Looking into your own cart, how full is it? Do you not feel the weight of your burdens you have been carrying? Life is easy if you just *let* it happen. Forcing things and following paths that are resistant to us, we must stop and reconsider. Is this what I really want? In time, by letting the Tao lead you to where you are supposed to be, you will avoid the long roads that you previously took. Our own desires can make us blindly push down these paths, filling our carts. By listening and feeling the Tao, it will naturally and calmly lead you to where you are supposed to be. In that place you will find happiness. There are no stones for you to pull here. It all begins with the desire to change. It is up to you to make it happen.

In our lives, we will be forced to bear many stones, despite our best efforts to keep them out. But even in these difficult times, we have the option of perspective to see just how heavy they really are. If in our minds they are so large as to fill our cart to the top, then surely we will stop in our tracks. It becomes so large in our minds; it is all that we can see. Though we cannot stop these things from entering our lives, we can truly influence their impact on us. A Taoist would view the same problem as a small stone, carried but insignificant.

"How can this be, this tragedy and sorrow I face is very real!" Yes, it is. It also is very real for the sage as well. The difference is in how she views it. A Taoist looks at the huge problem facing her, and begins walking backward. In a matter of moments, it shrinks in the distance, as the entire universe and her world around her come back into view. She now has the perspective to accurately and calmly face her problem with minimal effort, seeing the "Big Picture" in her minds eye. Her cart is very light indeed! If she views it in any other way, it will impact her more than it should, and bring her even greater difficulty. Her own problems are insignificant. Her own life is merely dust in the wind. She seeks only to be one with that wind.

As we continue on in our walk through this life, let the perspective of a calm and open mind show us our true loads that we bear. Our goals should focus on our own inner peace, which can only be found not in our own self-interests, but in holding open the door of the Tao. Here we find a tranquility that allows us to pass beyond the limits of basic human understanding. By keeping our problems in this light, we are focused on the "Big Picture" and not on the human condition. May we always have the serenity to understand not only all that we are, but our place in the universe around us. Once conquered, the cart remains a relic of our past, left now forever behind us.

The Whirlpool

Consider the people of the world as a huge pond. Every individual represents just one molecule in the pond. Every time we perform an unselfish act of love, we impart a push on the object of our attention and get it to move. This movement is very small, almost undetectable, yet it is a beginning. The person who receives this act may feel this love and impart their own "push" on another "molecule" thus starting a chain reaction.

Let's say then that these movements begin to form a pattern, a direction, defying the stagnant beginning of the pond, which represents despair, hopelessness, and darkness. This begins the journey of the current. When enough people begin reacting positively through the force of love, it is the whirlpool returning to you the reflection of a portion of the love you put into it.

Now the entire pond is capable of becoming a huge whirlpool, but it responds to natural resistances that exist in mankind's nature. Some people are not capable of pushing into the currents of the whirlpool, and cause a drag for those of us who are trying to accelerate it. We can flow around these circumstances by carrying them with us despite the resistance they cause. In time, we often "break them loose," bringing them along with us!

There are those that recognize the benefits of the whirlpool, but only latch on to receive the love and excitement of the power it gives them, and when the people they are using run out of love because they are not seeing their own love reflected back to them, they lose strength, slow down, and fall out of the current and become stagnant, not knowing what happened to them. Like a parasite, these people suddenly depart, and begin seeking another in the current to draw from.

We all need the love we put into the current reflected back to us. It is the natural power of the Tao in each of us that gives us the feeling of fulfillment and peace. The power of the currents and the whirlpools are all formed by the greatest power of all, love.

Now picture your own world, people that are close to you. These are "sub pools" within the overall huge whirlpool of humanity. We need these sub pools to get the reflections of our own love returned to us in an immediate response that keeps our daily lives motivated and happy. As you expand the power of the whirlpool, you will venture to give your love, knowing you will not immediately see its reflection returned to you. But it will affect others, thousands even! Think of it as a drop in the pond, the circle ever widening. Even after your work on earth is done, your effects in the whirlpool can continue on, even into forever. What an amazing thought! List your God and all of your favorite spiritual teachers or philosophers in your mind right now. Think of all the positive people you have met in your life. Do you not agree that the work they have done has changed the future itself, by their own selfless actions? The future is yours to shape, and you are the sculptor.

You matter. You make a difference in this world. Sometimes you can drop out of the mainstream, caused by a tragic event that draws all of your love away from you. You then slow down, returning to the stagnant beginning. It is very hard and sometimes impossible to find enough love and power nearby to propel yourself back into the mainstream. This is when you really need an infusion of love that can only come from someone close by. Close friends and loved ones serve this purpose. They can instill their love to you until you can slowly get "up to speed" in the whirlpool once again. Keep these people close at hand; you never know when you will need each other. Watch them and stay in touch, you will feel their speed in the current as it changes.

The whirlpool acts on everyone, even if they do not recognize it or actively pursue their own happiness. There are good qualities and traits in everyone, feel them as they give them to the whirlpool.

Start your own proof of this theory.

1) Believe in yourself. Accept yourself for who and what you are. You will become what you project. Try to become the very best person you can be. The stronger you become, the more power you instill in the whirlpool. The more of your love that is reflected back to you, the happier we all become.

2) Start with close friends and give of yourself unselfishly. Do not expect anything in return. In time, this will be your greatest treasure, because from it all of your rewards will follow. As you feel yourself strengthen, expand to strangers who you will take by surprise! You will carry each other faster in the current, and life will become fun again. You will be amazed on how large your little sub pool will grow!

3) Do not accept the canned definition of love that we have been taught by society. The Tao talks to us through nature and all living things. Sit down and watch them and feel the Tao as it passes through them to you. These will build and supplement your power in times of weakness, and help even out the surges in the whirlpool.

4) All negative thoughts and acts must be plucked like weeds from your lives. They only act to slow the current and reduce your happiness.

Celebrate your life each day. Treat it as a miracle. This will strengthen you and those around you until you become an overwhelming force in the whirlpool and achieve a level of happiness you never dreamed possible. Remember, from nothing you came, from everything you become.

Joseph Roggenbeck

Houses

In this chapter, I want you to close your eyes and picture a common image, in a very different way. Instead of viewing our own self-image in human form, I want you to think of yourself as a house. Within this house are many rooms. All are decorated uniquely and display your own feelings and emotions as you have traveled and lived in this home. The outside of your house is your body, and the clothes and person you display to the world every day. Each room in your house is a part of your personality, some explored, some locked until this moment in time. While we travel through life, we seldom really get a chance to know each other's rooms, let alone all of our own.

People are like houses. They are decorated and landscaped how the owners want the passerby to see them. They provide shelter from all the dangers of the world. As we build our fears, so we build our houses. We may put up bars on the windows, or take the front door right off the hinges. As you are beginning to realize, you have always been the master craftsman of who you really are, and how the world sees you.

Some homes are elaborate and decorative. Some are plain, even unkempt. But every house has a front door. Here lies the entryway. This is where the owner would greet the public. It is the only part of the house that is open to all. This is our "first impression." Actually it is our second, because most of us have already judged a little from the outside! As the old saying goes, don't judge a book by its cover. We should also be open minded when viewing others "homes." Keep in mind that these shells that are our bodies are merely a collection of our family's DNA. As the recipients of these cells, keep in mind that none of us was given a choice as to our body's appearance. We do however, have complete control over our minds. Remember this distinction when viewing the neighborhood.

Upon meeting and knowing people, we are allowed to see into other "rooms" of their house. These are personal reflections that they have chosen to share with you. By room, I am actually referring to areas of their mind. Some are lavish and beautiful, others cold and gray. Strong relationships allow us entry into other rooms of people's homes. In knowing the contents of the room, we have gained an insight into their own personal world. They have trusted you not to betray their inner feelings in letting you "see" inside themselves. Trust is a universal key, a very fragile one at that. Use it wisely, and you may have it for all time. One misstep and it can disappear forever. Walk softly while visiting in other's homes.

We decorate our rooms how we live our lives. When we find a beautiful and rich personality that is very compassionate for example, we have viewed a lavishly decorated area in this person's mind. When we find a person who is very self-centered, we have discovered a room that is very basic and in need of some remodeling.

It is a very close relationship that allows you access to rooms the owner keeps closed. Not everyone is allowed to see all of our rooms. Some are very personal and private. Others even we cannot enter. We need a key. Or we just need the right person to help us explore them. We travel our whole lives looking for these keys and people. Some live and die without ever knowing their entire house. How sad, being complete means understanding yourself. You never know who may give you a "key," or be that special person. Be open to everything! Discovering all your rooms is a very rich and building experience.

> "Ones own self conquered is better than all other people conquered; not even a God could change into defeat the victory of a man who has vanquished himself."
>
> *Buddha*

Take a look into your own house. Have you opened all of your doors? Are there a few rooms that you would like to fix up? Think of the people in your life so far that have impressed you the most. I am sure there are some ideas you can borrow from them in your own remodeling. It surprises me how many of us live in our "homes" our entire lives, with virtually no self-improvements! I have seen many fall into disrepair; these are very common, a result of destructive behavior and poor self-image.

But how great it is to find a palace to explore! I have toured a few of these homes, and I can tell you it is a life-changing event. The fact that the owner built them up brick by brick, with years of planning and overcoming setbacks of every type, is truly a beauty to behold. After seeing one, you will never view your own home the same way.

Don't be afraid to remodel. Anything can be changed. Seeking help during rebuilding is often a very wise decision. Experience is a very good teacher. Others will appear at the correct time. That is the power of the Tao. Whatever we need is readily at hand. You must trust in the synchronicity of all events.

At times, you may "fall down" in your remodeling, but don't despair. At other times you will make great strides! As you emerge into your new greatness, you will be amazed how others attract toward you! You may now have many tourists! Regardless of their understanding of it, the Tao will attract people. It is the positive energy you give off, it is your constant happy attitude. It is all the vast energy you now reflect, drawing them toward your "home." Essentially you will become a lighthouse, drawing people from all around you. They are seeking what you have, even though they may not actually know it themselves. Like the lighthouse, you will keep them safe from danger. As the sage reminds us, all are equal in understanding the Tao.

A good traveler paces the journey and arrives refreshed.
A good artist lets her intuition lead her where it may.
A good leader is free of preconceived ideas
And keeps his mind open to all.

Thus the sage is accessible to all people,

And rejects no one.
She is prepared for all situations,
And wastes nothing.
She carries the Tao within her.

What is a good man but a bad man's teacher?
What is a bad man but a good man's task?
To follow the Tao, you must know this, or you will be lost,
No matter how great you are.
It is the great secret.

Chapter 27 of the Tao Te Ching

Here, Lao Tzu is telling us that all people have value. Even if a man is so bad as to only serve as a bad example, he is not ignored. The sage must treat all equally; the Tao favors no one. By making use of it though, we can maximize its benefits.

Just as a builder plans his remodeling, so should you. Take the time to plan your work, and then work your plan. You are the carpenter, the bricklayer, and the artisan. Let the inside of your house be as beautiful as the outside! We all have the tools and the materials to build a palace—the choice is totally ours. It always has been. Until now, you have lacked the perspective this analogy has provided. Despite its simplicity, do not underestimate its value. It all begins again with those two simple words, "I can."

Control the future,
While it is still the present.
A tree as great as a man's reach springs from a tiny seedling.
A journey of a thousand miles begins with a single step.

Lao Tzu

The Sage in the Pond

There once was a great sage that was often seen by a small pond deep in the woods. In search of guidance, a king sought him out to find the source of the sage's contentment. Upon finding the sage standing motionless in the water of the small pond, the king called out.

"Oh great sage, the knowledge of your wisdom is known far and wide. I too seek its power. Can you show me the way?" Gently nodding his head, the man motioned the king toward him. The king could not swim, and he found the silt-covered bottom repulsive. Again he called out to the sage. "Come to me that you may then teach me your ways!" Again the sage smiled and motioned the king towards the pond. The king's fears could not be overcome. Why could the sage not just come to him? Having more important matters to attend to, the king left in despair.

Many weeks had passed when the king again returned to find the sage still standing quietly in the water of the little pond. The king was in great distress. His followers were abandoning him and armies were forming to challenge his country. He must have his answers now!

"Oh great sage, would you come to me and share your wisdom, that my country be spared from my enemies?" Once again the man gestured for the king to join him.

"But I cannot swim!" cried out the king.

"Nor can I," replied the sage. The king's desperation had now overcome his fears. Carefully he waded out to meet the sage.

"Can you now show me the way, oh great teacher?" whispered the king. His body was shaking violently. The water was now cloudy and the surface of the pond was alive with all of the movement.

"Look into the pond, for there lies the greatest wisdom a man can know," replied the sage. As hard as he could, the king looked into the pond, but he could see nothing but his own disruptions.

"Tell me, where is it!" cried out the king. The sage calmly replied.

"It is right before you my king." Unable to be still and patient, the king left again in desperation.

He returned to his home to find it had been overcome by his enemies. They chased him out, but the now dethroned king had escaped into the woods. He ran aimlessly for days. With no food, his clothing torn, and his body bleeding from running through the thick underbrush, the king finally collapsed.

Looking into a clearing, he could see a pond. Overcome by thirst, he drove himself forward. The king could not believe his eyes. Standing before him was the sage, still standing quietly in the water.

"They have taken everything! My kingdom is in ruins! I barely escaped with my life!" he cried out. Again the sage merely smiled and beckoned the king toward him. He suddenly felt a strange peace drift through himself. Could it not be too late? Is there still time? With new-found hope, he gently met the sage.

"Look into the pond, there lays the greatest wisdom a man can know," repeated the sage.

The king was now standing very still. With his kingdom gone and his home now in ruins, there was nothing left to fear. He stared into the depths of the pond. Suddenly, in his stillness, his own reflection appeared before him! In the background the beautiful countryside basked in the sunlight. With his crown and his clothing gone, the king studied his own face. This was once the face of a happy boy. He had not known fame, wealth or prosperity then, and yet he had been very content. It occurred to him that he had nothing now. He didn't need a kingdom to be happy! In that moment, the king knew himself. As a smile came across his face, he now understood the mystery of the sage!

When all was lost, in the depth of his misery, the king found his answers. With nothing left to lose, he finally overcame his fears. In the stillness, he found all he was ever looking for. The beauty that is the Tao was all around him. The sage had been using nature as a mirror. If he had only stopped and taken the time to see it! In our travels through life, be sure to take the time and see our own reflections. Ask yourself, "Is this who I want to be?"

Sometimes, we must be stripped of everything before we can rebuild. It is the force of change that propels us. As humans, we naturally resist change. We are comfortable in our jobs, our broken relationships, even our misery. When adversity sets upon us, we are forced to look at new ideas. Painfully we search for contrast and balance. Knowing this, we can now see how adversity is not necessarily a bad thing. It is a foundation for change. If we approach adversity with an open mind, it can lead you past a difficult path on your journey. Sometimes it is necessary to backtrack before we can find a new way. The mountain of life can be a very demanding mistress.

The pond represents life. If we seek answers from the depths, we must first be still. In stillness we can feel the Tao. Learn to be still like the sage. In tranquility lies your own true self. Know yourself, and you too shall know the Tao.

> "- not till we have lost the world, do we begin to find ourselves, and realize where we are and the infinite extent of our relations."
>
> *Henry David Thoreau*

Can you show patience and wait while the mud settles?
Can you remain still until the correct action is known?

From Chapter 15 of the Tao Te Ching

The Gift

In every adversity, and in every trial we are destined to carry, there is sorrow. This is a known predicament that is unavoidable in being human. The Buddhists call it being born into suffering. The great Dalai Lama tells us, "The day of your birth was the birth of your suffering." Nothing can shield us from the myriad of problems that we will face in a lifetime. Proper conduct and behavior will limit our self-induced troubles, but still, sorrow will enter our lives.

How do we react to this? We cry. We live in fear. We don a suit of armor to protect ourselves from future grief, while cutting off our connections to the living world. Many times, failure is accepted and the stone it becomes we carry in our hearts. It can become so huge we collapse under its weight. We literally carry it to our graves. We look to the sky and with outstretched arms we cry out to our Gods, "Why me? Is there no limit to what I must endure?" Even when the condition recedes, the source of our sorrow has run its course, and we carry it in our hearts as if new. What can be done?

After every sorrow, we must allow time to reflect. Take the time to closely examine all that has transpired. Play it all through in your head like a movie. Sometimes, we are still too caught up in the situation to be objective. We are wrapped so tightly in our problems, we cannot separate reality from emotion. In time, there is a point where we can examine what has happened to us. This is where the secret to uncovering the purpose of our experience is revealed.

Look for anything positive that can come from what you have just experienced. This is known as "opening the gift." By taking the good from the bad, we are turning a negative into a positive. If we fail to take the time to benefit from our sorrows, then we have suffered for no reason. By opening the gift, we are rewarded with new and positive things that we can use to build ourselves stronger. If this thought is new to you, these gifts are still laying behind you, all of them unopened! Take the time to go back and open them all! It gives a purpose to our lives if we can understand that adversity can be a positive thing. Only through these intense experiences can we find the tools to make us better, stronger, and better able to understand all that comes our way. Adversity drives change.

We can be too close to a situation to fully understand it. Like the eagle that soars far above us, we must see the bigger picture of what is going on. Think again of that person standing one foot away from a huge mural the size of a football field. In the beginning, we are too close to the situation to understand it. If every day we take a step back and continue to try and comprehend what has happened, in time we will understand the entire painting.

While watching my fellow companions in life, it became increasing obvious to me that they want immediate answers and accountability for all of their sorrows. There must be black and white, good and bad. Always we must want only the good side. But what of events that have no good side? I watch them stop in their tracks, and they suffer. It is the only option they have known. A Taoist smiles gently, and tosses the event into his pack, a small load to inspect later when time has finished nurturing it to its final purpose. Then he gently opens it later, and finds not a stone, but a dove inside, a gift for him that he releases to the world. Perspective has allowed him to lift the greatest of boulders, and carry them with no effort. There is a power here in this little story that not only can change your life, but all that you will affect in the future. A free and open mind that is compassionate to the world with no desires is the ultimate gift in this life. All other efforts have no value. You are merely existing for your own pleasures. If this key I give you has no meaning in your life right now, put it in your pack as the sage has done, and open it later when time has matured it. You will be amazed at what lays behind that door.

Be patient and continue to be optimistic in your travels. At some point you will come to the gift and recognize it for what it is. The gift is for you. It is meant to lead you, to teach you, and to comfort you. It may be hidden, but like a brilliant sunrise waiting for the passing of a darkened night, it will not be denied. Give it time to appear. It may not be readily apparent what the gift is. It can be disguised in many ways. Be objective while you wait. A gift can be found in any sorrow, let me show you an example.

I awoke one morning and could not talk. I had barely a whisper. My left arm had also become numb. I continued on my day, making an appointment with my doctor after several weeks of only minor improvement. Eventually, I was diagnosed with a tumor. Cancer! I was stunned. It was the second largest tumor my doctor had ever seen. Located in my upper clavicle area, it had encircled a portion of my heart, lungs, arteries, and had paralyzed my left vocal chord.

"Inoperable," he told me. I was in shock.

"What good could possibly come from this?" I asked myself. I quietly made my way to my car and thought about it—nothing. It was all bad, no matter how I viewed it. I was too close to the grief to be objective. It was too new—the gift was not ready to be seen.

The hardest phone call I would ever have to make, I called my wife and gave her the news. I was shaking as I pushed the buttons. I was coming home, but had to stop by work. My coworkers were compassionate and very supportive. I had an appointment the next business day with a surgeon. I have rarely been sick a day in my life, and now a surgeon? I could only picture in my mind how large the tumor was; five inches by three inches in diameter. That was the size of a brick! Nothing could rationalize the panic my wife and I shared.

At the same time, my wife had been struggling with Lupus, an autoimmune disease she had been diagnosed with for over ten years. She sometimes uses a wheel chair to get around in. Her complications had been escalating to the point of two hospitalizations in the past year, and monthly stays for treatment. She cannot work and fatigue severely limits her abilities and strength. Who would take care of us? I felt panic setting in.

I saw the surgeon on Monday. He was very reassuring and confident. He would take a couple of biopsies, and I would be out of the hospital the same day. There was a chance they would have to perform a more involved procedure, but that would only require an additional stay of two days, no problem. We went home to pack and get ready. I arrived the next day ready to begin a long battle; somehow I just knew it. It was September 11, 2001. I heard the news of the terrorist attacks on the radio on my way to the hospital. "Dear God," I said to myself, "pray for us all."

Just before surgery, I received a sedative. My responses were becoming slow and I was becoming groggy. I could see something was wrong looking at my wife. She seemed distraught. I told myself she was panicking about my surgery and passed out. I awoke two days later.

The pain drugs had made me very ill. It took forever for me to have any cohesive thought. I was told Cindy had been admitted for a heart rate that could not be controlled. With all of the drugs needed to control her disease, an interaction had removed the ability of the heart to regulate itself. Her heart rate had exceeded one hundred and seventy beats per minute! No matter what they tried, the condition continued to worsen. "Oh no!" I moaned. Then I looked at my chest. I had four incisions and a chest tube hanging out. "What is all this?" I demanded. I could not believe it! I felt like a truck had driven over my chest. My procedure had developed several complications. I had thrown a clot in my neck and blood flow to my left arm was severely restricted. It was to be seven days before I left the hospital; my wife also was discharged that same day.

I was told I had to undergo four months of chemotherapy for lymphoma, and six weeks of radiation. But the good news was that the cancer was confined to just the one tumor. My bone marrow tests had come back negative. "Now there's a start," I told myself. Now I had something to begin with. My one vocal cord is useless, but I could now speak again. Once more I was grateful for the fragment of sound that I could still use. Some voice was better than none. The fear of never being able to speak again was subsiding. It is amazing how fast your life can change, and I thanked God for his mercy.

Then it began. My family had taken on all of my duties. They emptied trash, drove us to appointments, cut my grass, closed my pool, and cooked us dinners. Endless phone calls from friends and acquaintances put us in touch with so many people! Emails were in the dozens every day. Baskets of gifts and flowers arrived almost daily. People I had not even talked to in years were filling my mailbox with get-well cards. Friends from my previous job had taken up collections and stopped by my home. They even came over and put the transmission back into my daughter's car that I had started before I was diagnosed! I received a long overdue phone call from my brother whom I had not heard from in years. Neighbors brought meals over on a rotating basis for months on end!

It was truly a tidal wave of love falling over us. I was absolutely speechless at the intense power of affection that was constantly flowing toward us. Despite the chemotherapy, the surgery, and my own fears for our health, this tremendous outpouring continued to build. I had never experienced anything like this before in my life. Being a very independent and private person, the cancer had stripped me of my independence and forced me to sit back and let those that would, love us. The outpouring of affection brought tears to my eyes. I had no idea we were so fortunate to have so many friends. I now was daily writing to people that had been only acquaintances. I had many heartwarming discussions with my family with whom I had suddenly gotten very close. The universe had reached out and supplied me with everything that I needed, and then some. In the moments of my darkest hour, these angels descended on my family and cared for us. I knew right then that I found my gift.

"The dove had emerged from within my pack, and what a beautiful sight it was, to set it free."

In our daily lives we touch so many people. I had never drawn on this power before. I had no idea how huge a circle of friends we had woven. When they came to our rescue, it was truly a sight to behold. The whirlpool continued to carry us, despite our inability to put back into it. My companions literally carried us upon their shoulders. I am very close with many of them now. The life threatening disease has brought us all closer together. We all have learned something about each other. In seeing the effect of all of this outpouring, I was able to rise up out of my battered body and appreciate the greatest gift of all—unconditional love.

While cancer is something I am glad to be leaving behind, I am not sorry to have had the experience. I took the challenge head on, and walked away the victor. This gift was not totally ours either. I cannot tell you the extensive impact it had on many around us, to see my wife and I carry our burdens together. Honestly, they walked away literally shaking their heads. Sometimes the gift is meant for many. To my dying day, I will have the confidence that I defeated that monster that would have destroyed me. I fought because my work here was not yet complete. I wanted to get this message to you. It is that important to me. I now walk with so much confidence I fear absolutely nothing. It has brought me so much closer to so many people; it has changed me in many ways. The gift in this story I will hold near my heart forever.

In time, I had something very positive to come from a potentially very negative experience. Gifts come in many forms. Be patient and watch for them. The ability to "open the gift" is a truly wonderful experience. It helps the world make sense. There is purpose in every action of fate, even if we do not immediately recognize it. In the great Tao, everything is balanced, even if we do not immediately understand it.

The road to our final passage in life takes many a winding turn. Our destinations lie not beyond our journeys, but within them. The sage sees the future within the present. In his detached objectivity, he finds in the darkness, secrets hidden by the light. Both unveil the master within, transformed by adversity, illuminated by the gifts received, and delivered to a future, which he has built today. Open your gifts in life; they have been waiting patiently for you in a future that is here right now.

The Mountain

Taoism is symbolized by a person running down a path. The ancient Chinese visualized this as life's journey. Now picture a mountain in your mind. It is immense! Its peaks extend past the clouds, the crest invisible to the naked eye. There are many paths that lead to the summit. None are easy. All have their unique challenges and solutions. Some lead to impenetrable obstacles.

The base of the mountain represents the beginning. It is easy to traverse; our choice of a spiritual existence begins here. The peak represents our final destination. It is the culmination of all the hard work we will endure in our passage. True peace and contentment, and the genuine awareness of all that surrounds us, await us here.

As we are born into this life, we begin a journey. Mature adults and experienced elders have their extensive history of their past to guide them. By using the benefits of their wisdom, they effortlessly climb. The answers they seek are not at the base. The farther they climb, the more they learn. As new levels are reached, new challenges and experiences await. They continue on, ever seeking knowledge and wisdom. As young children soon learn, they need guidance to climb the mountain. Because they lack the perspective from their limited experience, they have nothing to compare it to.

Adolescence is about exploring. Attitudes and ideas are changed like clothing as they run through the closet of their known options. They try on different costumes to see how they fit. Some they grow tired of, some no longer fulfill their current interests, and they don new attitudes and behaviors in search of their answers. But foremost, they are seeking answers. They are trying to define themselves. I'm sure your own past has many examples of this. Until they "stabilize" into a form of acceptable behavior, we use rules to guide them. These are limits to protect them from themselves. Exploring is a necessary tool, but it can be a perilous one as well. We all try to safe guard our youth; their innocence makes them vulnerable to many of the dangerous paths we have already been down.

But what happens then? After we are adults and have been given our own freedom to choose, we ask ourselves "Why am I not happy?" Do you remember thinking how everything would be so great when you got older? As we solved the questions of our youth, new problems came forth to challenge us.

Picture your spiritual journey as a climb up a mountain.

When we first begin to seek more from life than self-gratification, when possessions and early shallow life goals fail to sustain our happiness, we leave the foothills of our youth behind. You have chosen to rise above, to seek the unknown.

As we travel, we meet many people upon the path. These are others like yourself who have chosen to find what else is out there. The paths to true freedom in your soul lies somewhere up that mountain. Your answers may be close by or far toward the peak. All of us have slightly different answers to who we are and why we are here. The search for knowledge is a very noble and perplexing task. Rest assured though, you will meet many others on your journey. Some are not traveling upward though. Some seem to just travel a parallel around the circumference. They have reached a level of awareness, but are held back. They may lack guidance, or are being misled by a failed support system.

We all have support systems. We have built them over time. A support system can be anything you do to help you over a crisis. If it worked once, it will work again, right? So they continue on, hoping to keep it all together. Most of these systems fail at some point. They lack the depth of encompassing all of the infinite number of problems that a person will face in their life. So here they are unable to climb, but not wanting to return to their former selves, they have come too far for that. They have begun their spiritual journey, but are unable to proceed. That's one thing about the journey. Once you experience even a fragment of the serenity know as the Tao, it is like seeing a miracle, or meeting a God. No matter what happens, it is a life-changing event. It cannot be forgotten. It becomes an addiction to seek out the whole enigma, the truth that you now know it to be. Nothing you experience after that will replace that memory. The attraction will find you wanting to know and feel the depths of its vast and alluring seas.

You will have company on your path, no matter which you choose. There will be a time when someone appears in your life with goals very much like your own! You will share your experiences as you both make your way. Perhaps you will even open a door for them, or they will help you explore a room in your "house." Ultimately though, you both have your own destinations. The next day you may find yourself traveling alone again, only higher. Perhaps your paths will cross again higher on the trail.

Again I ask you to look into your memory, and list the five greatest people you have ever met. Now try to list the reasons why they were so great. You will find a common theme among these people. They *cared* about you. They attracted your feelings by being special. In each of them, there are a few traits you may want to model for yourself. It was this memory that was their gift to you. Use it in your climb, a tool for the future, from a loved one in your past. The Tao flows in balance through time, bringing us what we need, readily at hand, and with no effort. The door to a land of infinite beauty has opened wider with this understanding.

We will forever miss our spiritual companions as they come and go out of our lives. They left an invisible trace on our hearts as they pass through our lives. American Indian legend believes that once the parting of two special spirits takes place, that each soul now travels with a piece missing, now a permanent part of their departed companion. You have affected each other forever; a permanent mark on each other's spirit. You both will be forever changed. There is a sacrifice and a price to be paid in spiritual growth. It is the balance of the Tao working just the way it always has. It gives us perspective. It is teaching us to be humble. Learn to accept this as you climb.

In the distance you may see travelers much higher than yourself. These are the sages who have found many of their answers. If only you could reach them, and ask them some questions! Wouldn't it be so much easier! But the mountain is not subject to leaping forward. There are no shortcuts, and remember that their answers may not be your answers. You would not understand their teachings because you have not arrived at their level of comprehension yet. Be content with how far you have come. Remember, not all choose to climb.

There is a beauty in turning to face the descent of where you came. You can look back and see all that you have accomplished. You will see those far below, just beginning on their own climb up the mountain. How far you have come! It will take your breath away. Your new perspective lets you see farther than you ever have before. But your view skyward is very restricted. The future is not for us to see. We can only be prepared for what we will meet on the next crest.

Don't forget to mark your trail as you travel. Getting lost is very easy. A heavy storm or life changing event can wash you down the face of the mountain only to have you begin again. Crisis in our lives brings no warnings. A phone call can change your life. In times of turmoil, our emotions tend to take control. In time, we will have to sit down and rationalize these events. By writing down descriptions of your travels, and things that have helped you climb, you are essentially "tying off" your safety lines. In moments of weakness, your "maps" will bring you reassurance and definition. Keeping a journal of your growth can be a great source. Take notes from passages of favorite books you have read. Keep these close at hand. Take ten minutes on your lunch hour to review them. They will give you an amazing amount of strength and help you stay focused. Write down the names and titles of your favorite literary inspirations. If you truly seek positive change in your life, you will find that you have to work at it. You are worth it. You deserve all the happiness that is waiting for you. Only you can make it happen. Use these tools to guide you. These have become your footholds on your climb. They will lead you back, should you need them. Follow the Tao, and you will never be lost.

These will also serve as teaching materials for your students. One cannot follow the Tao without also becoming a teacher. All will come to the one. You have something special in you that they recognize as wanting for themselves. They may not understand it, but they feel it within you. It is a power that radiates from you, and many will recognize it.

Some may want to "latch on" to you. They want the light that you give off for themselves. Others want to emulate it, that they may carry it in their own lives. Be wise in this distinction. One is the student, the other a precarious follower. The sage lives to help all. There is a limit to what you can do. You may plant the seed, and water it, but you are just a messenger. The Tao brings everything to fruition. Things will take their own natural course. It is a wise sage that knows when a student can be taught no more. In the end, the student must do the work; only then will they know the master. Do not be led astray in your humbleness. It is wise to know exactly where you are, and how you got there. Should you need to retrace your steps, your records and journals will help point the way. Remember this on your own journey.

As you reach new levels, you will be overcome with joy! At times, your happiness will be overflowing. Others will ask you why you seem so content and in control. While it may be tempting to tell them all about your travels and goals, most are not ready yet to understand this foreign concept. Remember, the sage is humble to the world.

Let your image portray your own convictions. If your followers continue to ask probing questions, speak in generalities at first, assessing their intentions and level of commitment. Surprisingly enough, you will also now have followers! Only those ready to hear the teachings will listen and understand. Others will become confused and may even reject you! Your goal is your own spirituality. We must respect their current views. Your answers may not be their answers. Only when you are convinced of the student's sincerity should you explain your goals. Give them just a small view of your true inner self.

This is known as spreading the seed. It is difficult not to jump up and down and tell all the world of your happiness! You feel everyone should know what you know, to experience your new understanding of the universe. It is a humble person indeed who goes back to help others through the journey up the mountain. When you return to your travels, you may find yourself even higher than when you left!

Teaching reinforces our own understanding of the Tao. Students ask pointed questions that force us into new thought. Remember, the student may surpass the teacher. A great tree can emerge from such a small seed! In a lifetime, you may create vast forests. The beauty of the Tao is endless.

I wrote this poem many years ago when I first began peering into the magnificent ocean of the Tao. Though only wading, you can get a sense of just how intense the impact of its life changing powers had on me. Though I have since explored miles of its coastline, the vast depths of its ocean remain unexplored to me. How fortunate can a man be to wake every day and have this world to discover. Once we experience the Tao, a lifetime seems too short to know it all.

The Journey

The Machine of fellow man, his primal needs churn a deafening drone.
A tragic gray shroud of emptiness envelops my senses - I am blinded.

To stay is to perish, a hollow living death of no reward.

205

In the distance appears a mountain, majestic in its immense, dark and silent stature, it waits.

Drawn to its embracing danger, lies a foreboding solitude, calling, beckoning, a challenge to become. Am I alone in this quest? Have none gone before?
With my first step, I climb.

The foothills approach and fall away, passing like ocean waves beneath this faltering body that carries me upon this journey.
And yet still I climb.

The horizon looms ever larger. With every passing step, the terrain becomes treacherous and unforgiving. I fear failure awaits every foothold, every clutching grasp.
And yet still I climb.

An eagle careens past, challenging the sky itself. On the edge of control, it dances with the Gods. In contrast with my slow tedious progress, its freedom is inspiring, captivating.
And yet still I climb.

Jutting crags of confronting reality and the cold hollowness they bare, strip my flesh as I stumble, a monument to my passing.
And yet still I climb.

The wind has now become but a whisper, the silence becomes but a sound. My soul transforms my consciousness.
And yet still I climb.

The world is a speck below, the heavens loom ever larger. In this place I find my final peace that my life I've sought to know.
And yet still I climb.

JR

The Train

In our busy Western lives, there is an illusion pervading our society that leads us continually in a destructive and distracting cycle. It has no intentional misgivings. It was created and nurtured with only success and our own best interests in mind. The growth and advance of our civilization formed many ideals and desires of life that provided us with an image that was so much better than what we have known. It is our own human nature to try and improve our situation to our own advantage that drives this engine forward. Unfortunately, our lives and exhausting work ethics are the fuel to the boiler, and the engine continues to pull us along the track of illusion. By the time we realize a tragic and twisted life has been built for us, and that we are actually a captive member on a runaway train, it is too late to escape and we suffer.

Again I would like to use your imagination once more. It is the most powerful tool known to us, and I would like to turn the volume up, and redirect your current thoughts to a simple yet amazingly vivid window into my mind.

Imagine ourselves as passengers on a train. From our earliest memories, we have traveled only within its confines. Within the train are all of our daily requirements to live. Our schools, our jobs, our families, and all of the complications associated with them we carry on our trip on this train. We actively work hard to complete all of the tasks given to us, for we have been given this model that the train must go on. It uses our energy and our lives for fuel, and we blindly give our all to it. It is the only process we have ever known, and we are quick to defend it. The train is great! It takes us to new advances man has never known! It is the culmination of all that man has ever produced, and how proud we are to be a part of it! Everyone lives this way!

As we continue to tout its benefits and exploit the advantages to provide fulfillment to our own desires, we begin to question in the corner of our minds the mission that we have been given. As we begin to use a little of our own objectivity, we notice subtle details in the train that we have previously overlooked.

The train speeds up. The train slows down. As we work tirelessly and put our shoulder to the wheel that our lives may succeed, all that is outside the train is a blur, and we cannot observe the surroundings that the train passes through. We reach the end of our journey, yet we do not know where we have been. Occasionally events force us to stop working so hard. This also is the cycle of the train. When we rest from our tireless lives, and stop feeding the train with our blood and sweat, our train slows down naturally. Now we can observe the beauty and experience all of the events and gifts that wait quietly and in perfect contentment and natural synchronicity outside for us to explore. To view them and see them through the window of the train is the first level of awareness. We see a world much different from our own, and the attraction slowly becomes overwhelming to hold it for ourselves!

To walk away from the train and to sit down and suddenly see reality for all of its beauty and joy is the second level of awareness. But the whistle blows, and board we must, for our lives are intricately built into the structure of the train and we are swept aboard. Once again we are carried away in its endless churning and authority that we have given ourselves to. Within the train, we have built our lives, and within these are moments and periods of happiness that we truly experience and enjoy. But the engine demands our time, our energy, and with that our lives. The years pass by, and before we know it, we realize the train has taken us in a large and endless circle.

The decision to step off of the train is monumental, and a critical stage of our existence. It is a leap of faith. While frightening at first, we are driven by the desire to truly understand our lives, who we are, and where we are going. Once outside the train, we see a hulking smoking beast that would call us home. We have seen his tracks, and know his destination. It is human folly that built that beast, and the tracks that guide it. To be one of the rare, pure and beautiful people who understand and see this for themselves, we must congratulate, celebrate and rejoice in our uniqueness.

Every man and woman can recognize the train and see its power over them, but few can overcome its power with the one power that is greater than all, and is possessed deep inside all of us. It is the natural cycle of the universe and the peace and tranquility that quietly calls out to our senses, that we are connected to the entire living world; the sky, the woods, and the full moon outside our window. The wind that softly blows across our face, and the gentle heat of the sand under our feet all are whispers of subtle manifestations, like the smell of a rose, that brings us a satisfaction that was never quite explained to us. We were too busy on the train; feeding the engine, wasting our existence. Here we have in our hearts for the first time, once free of the train, felt the Tao.

We must never go back that way again! But the train is intrinsically tied to us. Though we did not build it, our birth within its walls has forged obligations we need to complete. These are not all bad things. We can have good marriages, jobs, hobbies or interests that help us complete our existence and in that process, mature as humans as the cycle of life completes its course. So we travel once more in the train, but this time with an objective and detached picture in our minds. We have found that all is not what it seems. There is a peace, a world, and a beautiful force of contentment that we have felt for the very first time, and we know somehow that we must have more of it in our lives.

But how do I live in both worlds? They both draw me in, and I cannot exist in either without some complications! How true this is. If we were to spend our total existence off of the train, we would be like wandering monks, with no visible means of supporting ourselves. Though this is an option that some would sacrifice it all to keep away from the train, the Western world has neither place nor compassion for these sages, and their ability to be content cannot be maintained. This is an unfortunate condition of our world today, but a reality nonetheless. We see the train and know that we must board. We are intrinsically tied to it and it to us. What a strange existence we have been born into. Looking out the window as we travel once again, there surely must be a way to have it all.

The world outside our train windows gets dark at times. We find events within our lives that are beyond our capability to handle. We look outside the train for external guidance, but it is dark, and there are no answers forthcoming. In these times, events have been brought for us to learn and grow from. While painful and heartbreaking, we progress in our spiritual development, that we have some depth and level of awareness to our lives.

Other times the light outside the window of our train is bright, and the sun is out brilliantly! Our hearts are at peace and we enjoy all that was meant for us. This is the great cycle of the Tao! We see the entire spectrum of events that surround us, and take it all in with the understanding that things will endlessly repeat themselves.

I have seen many men, in their belief that the train held the answer to all of their desires, leap onto another train that was passing! In this faster train, he works even harder, and looks out of the window even less, waiting for the next faster train to arrive, that he may continue on in his search for completeness.

We sometimes wish for a different existence, and on this path we take a risk. But we choose from our own desires, and this path leads us to leap into another train, one heading in any other direction than the one we were going. In time we find that while this was indeed a change with both positive and negative benefits, life still is incomplete, and the engine draws its due.

Fast trains are expensive. Their board is paid for in time. A man's life and blood are taken, and deception is the dollar exchanged by the train. Even if a man survives the route, he has failed. Time cannot be bought by any measure, and the experiences meant for us are lost. The route cannot be traveled the same way again.

Look for the train that is traveling slower than yours. Watch carefully. Calculate the jump. Take the chance. It is the one opportunity to get closer to being truer to yourself. Its engine requires less of your time, your sweat, and your energy. Now you have the chance to look out the window, roll it down, and take in the fresh air and feel more of life than you have ever known. Now we have the option of stepping off of the train! It continues on ever slowly, but we can catch up with it in time and complete the details of our lives that we are bonded to. We feel alive! This is the Tao. It has existed outside your train forever. Only by walking in it and understanding its mysteries may we truly feel contentment in our hearts and know the real cycle of life. This is the world within your world. Though we may have glimpsed it on occasion, the train has kept us distracted from ever reaching it. Wave goodbye to the faster trains that would beckon us in their false attractions. The glitters of their gold plated interiors are an illusion once we have seen the cold dark hulking metal animal that they truly are. Once we put all the pieces together, the picture becomes very clear.

In my own life I must ride the train, but continually keep an open eye to the window. Whenever I am able to, I step off the train, and watch it pass by. Suddenly I hear the birds, feel the wind, and taste the sweet scent of the trees that give their gifts to me. While I know I must ride the train, I do so as slowly and with the least amount of effort that I can. What

I refuse to pay the train in the gold that has become my time and my life, I give to the world, that we may all one day spend more time here and forever enjoy our own self-won freedom.

Your fellow travelers on the slower trains you will find most interesting as well. In their company you will discover warmth, beauty, and compassion in depths that will draw you ever deeper. They too have found the secret of the slower train. In their personal rediscovery, the beauty of the Tao radiates through. What a beautiful ride we now enjoy in this life! These are your riches now. You have made the trade of a lifetime.

We must board our slow trains when the whistle blows, but we now live our lives in a normal pace, with peace, understanding, and contentment. Perhaps one day we may reach a point where the tracks end. I hope one day to have slowed my train down to this point. Every man and woman should hold this picture in their minds, a constant reminder of our pasts, our futures, and where they should be leading. Here the mystery of the Tao waits patiently and endlessly for us.

To travel to where man has not, we must begin where his tracks have ended.

As I wait outside of the train for those that have "slowed down," I hope to have pulled you if only for a moment off of your train and into my world. I assure you that those around me are among the most beautiful and incredible humans you have ever met. A Taoist has patience and understanding beyond measure. Here I will wait for you.

Synchronicity

One day I had been out walking, and entered my favorite bookstore. My recent studies had been reinforcing the practice of synchronicity. I had decided that in order to advance the power of experiencing the Tao more deeply within my life, I must give it the opportunity to show itself more spontaneously in my daily travels.

I walked ever so slowly and with an open mind to many different places in the store. When the whim hit me, I would pick up a book and examine it carefully, no matter what the topic. As I continued, I began to get a unique urge to move toward the clearance table. As I allowed the feeling to expand, I found that as I moved toward the very lower shelves, it became stronger. I felt a little silly as this process progressed. I was wondering if there was really much value to this approach and began to chuckle at the thought of how humorous it would appear to the outside observer.

As I lightly touched the different volumes though, it was very obvious that my mind was somehow going through a process of its own. When I had reached the very last book, at the very back of the bottom shelf, a subtle yet obvious feeling had come over me. I had found it. I had yet to know even what "it" was, but my open mind had arrived at its own destination and I was now to try and understand the synchronicity of this little adventure.

215

I read the title out loud, "*Mutant Message*—by Marlo Morgan." Curiously I read the preface. It was an original true story of a woman who had followed her own synchronistic instincts all the way to Australia to find herself on a trip across the continent with an Aboriginal tribe. Here she discovered more about herself in four months than she had known in a lifetime. What an incredible story! The book was also on clearance for less than five dollars! But my reward for following my instincts had not yet finished revealing all that this trip would bring to me.

As I walked up to the counter to pay for my gift, a young man at the register greeted me with a curious smile.

"Good Morning!"

"Hello!" I returned his greeting and smiled back.

"Did you find what you were looking for today?" he asked.

"I believe I did!" I answered with a slight laugh. It was then that part two of my journey would be revealed.

"You are a Taoist aren't you?" the cashier asked me, still with his genuine full smile on his face. Surprised and awkwardly I responded.

"How could you possibly have known?"

"As you walked in, you had no preconceived destination. I watched you as you made your way about the store, visiting areas most men never enter. When you found what was waiting for you, you recognized it immediately and appeared to complete a mission within yourself."

"Surely there is more!" I responded. I was curious to know the answer!

"Your dress was very casual and basic. Your appearance was neat and clean, yet not overdone. You also have a very relaxed manner. You smiled as you met the other customers and talked lightly as they crossed your path."

"But there must be something else," I replied. Now it was his turn to laugh as he looked at me peculiarly.

"I felt strange as I came to work today. I knew something unique was going to happen. As I have trained myself to follow my instincts, I watched closely as this simple man quietly influenced his surroundings. It could not have been more obvious to me that you were a Taoist, for you see, it takes one to know one."

I was stunned as he quietly explained his observation with me. I had only met one other Taoist in my life, and yet today, another had made himself known from merely watching me! I found this utterly amazing. This was my first adventure with synchronicity, and the power of how it can change your life could not have given me a bigger lesson that morning.

The final piece to this puzzle was the book itself. I found it very moving, genuine, and one of most wonderful stories I had ever read. It is today one of my treasures, and has since traveled through many hands.

What an interesting life I had yet to live from this moment forward! When we walk with an open mind, and free our hearts of preconceived ideas and emotions, we allow the Tao to supply us with many gifts. How long had I been missing them?

I have since had hundreds of experiences like the bookstore. It seems unlikely, doesn't it? But experiencing is believing. With it my entire life has changed. I had allowed the power of an open mind to unlock a door in my life and allow the universe to quietly slip in and take me with it. In search of my own desires and interests, this door had previously been closed.

To sum a Taoist view of the world, he lives only in the moment. Yesterday is history. It is used only to view our mistakes that we may learn from them. Tomorrow is wrapped in ambiguity. It may hold good things for him or bad. He does not care either way. In accepting that life is a river of turns and rocks, he knows where he has been, and that in time, the river will flow peacefully once again. A Taoist is the eye of the universe. By not following all of man's daily distractions of his own worldly desires, he is now free to merely watch and experience the living world. How he appears in the eyes of others is insignificant. Compared to the beauty he sees all around him, his own vanity is transparent. He has no anxieties about his future. The current of the Tao will steadily take him to where he is supposed to be, effortlessly and with no concerns. He lets life happen. He knows that by forcing and acting on desires, they will only lead him to difficulty so he lets them go and watches as they disappear, no longer a chain to hold him.

In living only in the moment and with no concerns of himself or his future, he is truly free, and watches the world, the universe, and the Tao as they flow naturally to him. This is known as synchronicity. Incredible events and gifts wait for us in our lives. While some occur and are ours to enjoy, we frequently overlook all of those that were meant for us.

"How can I know what to do or when to do it? If I take a chance, I can get hurt, rejected or embarrassed." Yes these are possible, but your current method of making choices has not resulted in all that you have wished, has it? Because a Taoist believes in balance and has placed no desires on her world, making choices can appear very curious to the outsider. Because she believes the correct thing will happen at the correct time, she embraces every event, be it Yin or Yang. With this way of thinking, a detour on her way to work is a chance to see some sights she has been missing. Or perhaps it led her away from a traffic accident she would have been involved in had she taken another route. Though she may never know the real reason, it really doesn't matter. She enjoys whatever comes her way, for it is meant for her. She pulls up into her parking spot and meets a stranger who gives her a smile and a warm "Hello!" The river of life has brought this small gift for her to enjoy. Most people would be so distracted by the disturbance of their normal routine and being late for work, the gift is washed away, the moment of synchronicity vanished.

For a Taoist, every day is a leap of faith. Decisions are made based on her feelings and gut instincts. She is tuned to the entire fabric of life, thus her objectivity is rewarded with a continual flow of gifts, happiness, and amazing events that we used to see as "chance." In tune with the Tao, she knows what to do, and when to do it. No could have, should have or what ifs. Once the decision is made, she never looks back or second-guesses herself. By allowing for the synchronicity of events to present themselves, and then walking through those doors into the unknown, she has taken a risk; a risk that she may rise above a mundane existence, a risk that her contentment will always be her own to control. Yes, this is truly a risk, a risk that we cannot afford *not* to take. To trust totally and with no reservations in anything in our existence is rare indeed. But our inability to be free of our anxieties and our own inhibitions trap us in a mundane and shallow world. When we live our lives with a little spontaneity, we allow the Tao to flow through us and feel the compassion of the universe. If we look at every event in our lives as an opportunity for events of satisfaction and happiness, then we find what we have been seeking. It is that simple. Once we train our eyes to see the patterns, we find it simple to recognize them now that we know what to look for. Let me follow this idea with another example.

I was unhappy with my career at one point, when a total stranger approached me with an opportunity. I could keep all of my job skills that I had learned, but had to severely cut my pay in exchange for some better benefits. I also would be entering the world of a huge corporation. I was very troubled with this decision. Such a huge risk! I desperately needed the cash flow to support my young family, and wanted to work for a small family business that knew and appreciated me. Finally I listened to my inner self and my instincts. If this person and opportunity came into my life, it was for a reason. I took the chance, and have never regretted it. Though not fully aware of all of the formal aspects of the Tao, I inherently had been following many of the concepts unconsciously for years. By quieting my mind and listening to the Tao, I allowed the gift to present itself and reward my life.

Years would pass when this exact same scenario presented itself yet once again; another total stranger with another career offer. I was content with my work, but felt unchallenged.

There was nothing left to conquer. My skills had topped out in my current profession and it was a dead end job for me now. Again I stood back and listened to the Tao. The synchronicity of all of the events that had occurred for this opportunity to take place was incredible. I had passed an extensive interview process, and realized that I would never have this chance again. The door was open and I had to decide.

I made a phone call with one of the staff at my potential employer that led to a series of conversations. This very warm and caring person on the other end of the phone sparked the feelings of synchronicity once again in my mind. I knew right then, that I had made my choice! I walked through that open door into the unknown.

While this may seem totally crazy to you, I forever knew that the correct decision had been made and there was nothing left to reconsider. It had become a total leap of faith. The results have been most rewarding, and my impression of that staff member was totally correct and vindicated upon our meeting, and has rewarded my life with her entrance into it. In my continued search for life's rare and truly remarkable people, I was rewarded once again by following my instincts. While some may use their lives to build their finances, belongings, or fulfill their own self-interests, I have chosen to search instead for those intense and wonderful people who are scattered out among us. The experiences are far more valuable than any reward I could ever receive. To have found another was a miracle I find hard to describe. Synchronicity again quietly and ever so gently had presented a gift for me yet again in my life. As I measure it, I am the wealthiest man in the world.

The doors of opportunity and happiness wait for us patiently. We need merely to understand their meaning and learn to open our minds to the natural synchronicity that was meant for us when they pass our way. As a man stranded in the ocean, any ship in passing was meant to be. We question not its direction or its constitution. Our lives are not as guided by chance or our own will as you would believe. A Taoist finds meaning in all events, and knows that good or bad, they have been meant for her. With no selfish desires or preconceived ideas on how life is supposed to be, she is free to embrace synchronicity and all that it would show her. The universe and the Tao that guide it flow steadily to the open mind that she has tuned her life to hear. In my own life the results have been miraculous without question.

The next time you have that urge to call an old friend, walk a different path, or pick up an interesting book from the shelf, think of this chapter. Events, people, and opportunities have passed us by in the river of life. With a new perspective, we may now recognize them, embrace them, and enjoy the gifts that have been waiting quietly for us. The Tao brings all things to fruition. How wonderful it is to just let them in!

A Taoist View

Taoists found in Western society generally were not raised to understand and learn their philosophy from birth. In searching for their answers in life, they, like myself have uncovered this frequently overlooked and hidden way of life known by the ancient Chinese as Taoism. But no matter what spirituality we serve in life, we must find it applicable to our daily lives. It must give us support and comfort that all in our lives has meaning and purpose. But spiritual guidance must be more than just words. It must be flesh and blood, heart and soul, your sincerest commitment to be the strongest person you can be, not just for yourself, but also for the world around you, which so desperately needs your guidance. That ultimately must be your destination. In serving your own desires, you prevent the miracle of giving yourself away and the absolute power and pure joy that it returns to you from fulfilling all of your needs.

You see we really don't need all of the things in life that we think we do. We seem to have bought this idea from modern society that in order to be successful and happy, we must fulfill this list of requirements. They are requirements, that much is certain. They have become requirements for your happiness and solitude. I have examined each desire in my heart and rejected these weights on my soul, and choose instead to travel my life with no such demands; the most open man whose gaze has ever held your mind. As a gardener weeds his garden, you too must look inside yourself, and consciously decide what you really need, and what you can do without. In the end, all that will remain is the beautiful garden that is you, in total simplistic beauty, as you were meant to be.

A Taoist makes do with what life brings. She enjoys it, watches it, learns from it and gives it away. True happiness does not lie in the things you get, it lives quietly in the seeds of your fruit which you throw to the wind, that all of your compassion may grow in your absence and return mature, beautiful, and satisfying to your heart. It all returns. That is the Great Secret. Let me show you what has been lost.

We have so many choices in this world today; what we eat, the clothes we wear, and the furniture we choose for our homes. What career should I begin? What car should I save up for? What area should I raise my family? With so many choices, we become inundated with options, questions, and desires to always want the best. But the best is never quite good enough. We tend to use objects and people to validate our lives. Before long we are caught up in this endless cycle of filling our lives with "things" and our search for contentment escapes our grasp. In trying to keep all of the balls in our life in the air at the same time, they begin to drop and the entire system winds up on the floor.

> "Why should we be in such desperate haste to succeed, and in such desperate enterprises?"
>
> *Henry David Thoreau*

In our want to have the best, we have left out of the equation the desire to *be* our best. What does being the "best" mean to you? For many, it is the grade on an exam, a college degree, or a successful career. Who sold you these definitions, that these values would make you something special, and why do we believe them? While our successes are important to our lives, they should not be our measuring stick for who we are. This is where we have gotten lost in our world today. Our careers are not who we are. The plaque on the wall does not make us a quality human being, worthy of respect. It is your personality, your attitude and your devotion to your fellow man and the deeds you perform that define the best you can be.

I know many of us do not live by that definition. We are good law abiding people. We raise our families, go to work every day, and generally do the best we can. But something is missing. There appears that relentless, nagging, and underlying call that whispers softly to you, that something is not right. A vacation, a new toy, or a new relationship will perhaps solve this for us. For a short time, the distraction works. But all of these distractions have limits. Very often, they do not solve our problems, but add to them! The voice is not content, and calls out yet once again. It is very subtle, but in our moments of despair, in our hours of sleeplessness it calls, and we continue to wander.

We have become disconnected from the Tao. It is easily found in nature, and many of us seek it out there. A day in the woods can be so refreshing. The beauty of a mountain valley stirs a unique chord in our hearts. That note is the Tao, playing quietly just as it has done forever. We long to stay here, where for unexplainable reasons, we feel much happier. That is the whisper of the Tao, gently touching you.

But we cannot live in the woods anymore. We are civilized. We are born into working for a living and sign up for all of the complications associated with joining civilization. This is all very normal and acceptable. It is unrealistic to go forth and live in the woods as Henry David Thoreau did, to live our lives in harmony. While the present is constantly changing, we must adapt and find new ways to apply old ideas. The value behind them is not lost, for goodness never goes out of style. We must learn to pick up and examine these spiritual artifacts, left for us on our journey through life, that we not repeat the same mistakes as our fellow humans, who searched and found these answers for us.

There are many truths and similarities in all spiritual systems. We tend to use those that have been handed down to us, or hold an advantage that fits our needs. The accompanying rituals are placed to constantly reinforce the message, along with many other elements that we begin to hold with suspicion. The Tao makes no such demands. It merely is. It has no conscience. Consciousness is the awareness of the self. Pure thought has no form. The self appears from its own needs. With no thought, there is no self. With no self, there is no conscious. With no conscious, there is only the purity known as the Tao. The way back to the Tao has been lost and the secret well hidden by all of our busy lifestyle demands. I hand the jewel of the Tao to you now, within the pages of this book, that you may hold it in your heart forever. To keep it safe, you must be the best you can, every day.

A Taoist believes that to be your best, you are invisible to yourself. You follow the simple rules of not wanting for your own desires. All that you ever will need is readily at hand. Just use the power of a positive and open mind to apply yourself to the tasks when they arrive. In being selfless, the heart is not distracted.

There is an endless selection of distractions that we choose to focus our energy and attentions on. It is so much easier (and self-centered) for us to tune into these tangents in our lives today. You may justify them any way you like, but ultimately they are mere rattles in the baby's playpen, designed to occupy time and mollify a wandering mind.

Our ancestors had few such distractions. Their energy was focused on survival. In living life close to the bone, they had a much deeper understanding of life and conversely were not so easily led astray. In living a basic existence, they understood and appreciated the Tao, nature, and all of the small things in life. The change of the seasons, the new moon, and a clear night sky, all drew their attention and were entertainment in their own simplistic way. When was the last time you laid outside and took in the night sky for hours on end? My point here is to bring you back to what is lost in your lives.

As you recognize the truths that I have demonstrated for you in this book, expand them and apply them to your own life. Begin by separating yourself from all of your desires. They only hold you back from all that you long to be. Objects are a paradox. The more importance we place on them, the more power we give them over us. It is a great man who can walk away from all that he owns, and his contentment stands as firm as the earth under his feet.

> "And when the farmer has got his house, he may not be the richer but the poorer for it, and it be the house that has got him."
>
> *Henry David Thoreau*

In the modernization of mankind, much more has been lost than what has been gained. If we live so much longer now due to advancements in science and medicine, of what value is it to us if we have been so disconnected from the basic elements of nature and the Tao, that we are miserable or discontented for the majority of our existence? We have come to depend on these objects and distractions so much, that they have become a prerequisite for our happiness. This is so very tragic.

The machinery that was going to give us more time, has paradoxically taken it away! We work harder now than we ever have. In our efforts to microanalyze every molecule and how it functions, the entire system of the Tao continues on, in endless motion, totally overlooked, following only itself. While we study the seed in the wood, an entire forest has grown to cover us.

Man cannot see the whole
Thus he must name the parts.
Names lead to science and study.
Science and study cannot lead to answers.
For the Tao divided
Cannot be found.

All things that know this, flow like great rivers,
Returning home to the sea known as the Tao.

From chapter 32 of the Tao Te Ching

As a race, we have changed more of the course of nature in the last fifty years, than the entire history of our planet. Many of these changes were dressed up and sold as "good things." The Nuclear Age brought with it advancements in medicine that has saved hundreds of thousands of lives, including my own. It also has been used as the ultimate weapon, whose shadow we will now live under forever.

There once was a madman who longed to rule the world. In his drive for absolute power, he directed his researchers to find a way to create the "perfect" race. Blonde hair and blue eyes were determined to be part of the standard. These armies would be superior to any other, thus solidifying total control "in the name of our country," and over his own people as well. The unified powers of the civilized world recognized this danger, and the horrors associated with it and defeated this evil force. While there were many other factors involved here, (such as occupying land that did not belong to them at an alarming rate) it was accurately recognized that this was not a good thing, and must not continue.

Now flash forward to today. We have test tube babies. We have experiments that have successfully cloned and began replication of human organs in test chambers. We have cloned animals as well as created genetic modifications to all manner of vegetation, fruits, and flora. I can assure you with absolute certainty, the human clone, genetically mastered to be superior and disease free, able to live longer and survive long periods of interplanetary space travel, genius level mental capacity and athletically perfect, is just around the corner. Many researchers outside of the United States have claimed to be working on this as you read these lines. It will happen. Once the genetic codes were unlocked by science, the proverbial Pandora's box was opened, and the human race must now bear the consequences.

But we are told, "This is a great day! The human race will benefit!" Let me tell you now, I believe it is the gravest mistake man has ever made. We claim to have the knowledge and understanding that we can control all aspects of science. We still cannot predict even the weather for tomorrow. The implications and the ramifications of genetic tampering cannot be undone, repaired, or justified to cover the consequences we as a race are going to suffer. Already, the first engineered corn has begun to wipe out an entire specie of butterfly. Laws against using this product in the United States are mere window dressing. A major brand food distributor was just found to have released it into our food supply, and we have already begun the destructive cycle that these actions are just beginning to show.

Man cannot be trusted. He has not the knowledge or integrity for what he is doing in changing our natural world. What will become of these super humans when they arrive? They are coming, rest assured. Only a source of great wealth will be able to afford them. So that leaves governments, large corporations, and terrorists in control of their use. Are you starting to get a little uneasy here? As we solve problems with science, we create others to take their place. The scale of the damage is increasing at an alarming rate. Sometimes it seems we are destined for our own destruction.

Genetic research is frightening, to be sure. But there conversely have been many benefits as well. The possibility of eliminating genetic diseases in our children, the future of organ transplanting, that we may live longer lives, all are balances to the other side of the equation I have just shown you. This also is the Tao! The negative and the positive continue on in this endless dance. Over two thousand years ago, Lao Tzu had foreseen these events, and left us this message.

Those that would change the living world will destroy it.
The universe is perfect.

Thus any change upsets the balance.
Those that seek to change it, will ruin it.
It cannot be held, as man tries to own all things,
For it will vanish.

So sometimes things are ahead, yet they are seen as behind.
Sometimes there is success, yet it can appear as failure.
Sometimes there is strength, yet it is perceived as weakness.
Sometimes what makes us joyful, brings another sorrow.

The sage watches all things,
Knowing their place is in perfect order.
Thus he achieves balance,
By leaving them alone.

Chapter 29 of the Tao Te Ching

I find this quite an observation for an unknown wandering man in China, over two thousand years ago. The power of the written word cannot be underestimated. It has traversed time and distance to provide us wisdom, that we may see our mistakes and correct them. Our future does not have to be dark. It can be anything we want it to be. Again I would have you read this most important quote for a second time.

"You must be the change you wish to see in the world."

Mahatma Gandhi

If we really want to make a difference in our future, then it must begin with understanding. Recognizing the knowledge of the Tao and its place in our hearts is the first step. Making it our reality every day that we may be happy and content and centered is the second step. Bringing our fellow humans back to what is lost, that they too may see these truths and understand them for themselves is the third step. The power of a simple and balanced life cannot be overstated. Once found, sharing it with others is rewarding beyond imagination.

There is much disharmony and suffering caused by our unfortunate disconnection to the Tao. Even Gandhi as great as he was, could not stop mankind from its path toward continual disharmony. This is understood and accepted by Taoists. We cannot change everything. Some things in life are predestined and have their own course. If we feverishly attempt to change the inevitable, then we too are pulled into the fire. We are the balance to the equation. In all the madness, all the confusion and sorrow and self-destructive behavior that goes on around us, we remain the rock that all may cling to. In the face of every adversity there is a Taoist smiling, because he sees it all, understands it all, and has come to complete terms with it within his heart. He does what he can do, with no predetermined ideas of how life is supposed to turn out. It is what it is. He sleeps peacefully, knowing tomorrow again will show him the beauty of the Tao, in all of its manifestations, and that he is now one with it.

In this chapter, you have probably found similar thoughts in your own mind, but never really put it all together before. In the mural of life, I have shown you your own image, hidden in the canvas! I have seen it all along, and now we share that.

Life is easy. *You just let it happen.* No forcing, no desires, no problems. The correct events will flow your way as you gently paddle your way down the stream of life. When the rapids come into your life, you will be ready, and move quickly when necessary, and return effortlessly to a calm state of mind that moves no faster or slower than is necessary. A Taoist adapts to any situation or life style, seamlessly. She makes friends wherever she goes. Not a harsh word can be spoken of her. Her actions continue to be honorable and selfless. When negative events enter her life, she treats them with any resources available with the understanding they hold hidden meaning and values, as well as positive energy. All things are possible, and the future is of no concern. Everything is just as it is supposed to be. She is in harmony with every object in the universe, connected once again with the Tao and its timeless cycles of perfect balance. This jewel, I give to you. When you live this way, life is everything you can ever imagine and so much more.

It has been said by the ancient Chinese masters, that a man who is at peace with his world sleeps a solid and rested sleep with no dreams or nightmares. He goes to bed and closes his eyes, and opens them with the dawn a fitful and rested man. Because he lives his dreams, they have been released into his world. Because he has no fears, there is no place for them to hide within his mind.

In my own life, I have found this to be true. But it was not always so. Before I understood the Tao, I dreamed many varied and vivid dreams and nightmares. I had many sleepless nights, and could not always settle my mind to embrace evening's quiet calling. But times have changed, and with it so have I. My whole life has taken on many different patterns. The quiet in my sleep is the manifestation of the quiet in my mind.

Look up in the night sky with me tonight. Think of all the galaxies out there, revolving, dancing in perfect order, being brought to life, disappearing into black holes and transforming again in an endless cycle of synchronicity. Our ancestors and every man who has ever walked the earth have all seen this great miracle and wondered of his own existence. Tonight, we share the understanding and purpose of it all.

Adrift

The Past is but a shadow,
A memory now set free.
The Future holds the promise
Of what may or never be.
It matters not what Fate has brought,
As we are tossed upon its sea.
These depths are not deeper
Than the beauty that lies
Deep inside of me.

JR

In the End the Dishes Must Get Done

So now that I have this new awareness, what now? My car still needs repair, the garden still needs weeding and the dishes still need to be done. Has anything really changed? Having an understanding of the Tao will not make the realities of life go away. Rather, it will help you understand how to cope with them and guide you in your decisions and actions. Bad things will still happen. Good things will still happen. This is all part of the great mystery. With practice, you will accept both equally. In understanding the Tao, there is no difference.

> "There is nothing good nor bad, but thinking makes it so."
>
> *Shakespeare*

The electricity will still go out. Disease will still affect your loved ones. Your teenagers will still drive you crazy. All of these will test your mental well-being. In times of stress, you will find yourself falling back into your old "ruts" of thinking. This is understandable. You have carried them with you your whole life—they have become ingrained in you. It was all we were ever taught in handling stress in our lives. But a greater understanding and constant practice of the Tao *will bring you back to center* quickly. Here we may now be logical, look for simple solutions, and see the situation for what it really is. We can never be truly free of our emotions. We will continue to give them some control over our lives. It is our choice though to limit these emotions that we may apply true perspective to our daily troubles.

The morning sunrise, the call of a cardinal, an intricate cloud formation, and a smile from a stranger—these things now have a measured depth in our new understanding. Life is not about keeping the "bad stuff" away, it is very much about appreciating *all* that we experience and recognize while celebrating the many small positives hidden in our days.

We do not need to see the wind, to feel it upon us. We accept that it exists as we watch the leaves dance on the trees, and see the fields of grain drift before us. Though we cannot hold it, we accept the manifestation as it moves through our lives. The Tao also is an invisible force that moves through all of life with an unseen hand. Like the wind, we see its manifestation, but not the source. When we have no understanding or awareness of the Tao, it is a very still and silent world we see. Our own needs and desires are all that are visible. When we follow the Tao, we see an entire universe in constant interaction, and feel our own presence within the great mystery. Here the wind brings many gifts and manifestations for us to enjoy! In my own mind, I see and feel the hurricane of its power, dancing continually around me. Thus my life is filled with abundance, as I continually watch it fulfill all of the destinations of the ten thousand things. In understanding the Tao, we now have a profound reflection of the world. Things make sense now! We find purpose and understanding in all of life's events—the good and the bad, the beautiful and the ugly, the depth of sorrow and the incredible brilliance of joy. It is all found as easily as the breeze upon our face.

As we have come into our own in these lessons from this book, I would like to impart to you one significant truth. As we understand the Tao and come to understand all of its mysteries, there is a point where there needs to be more than just an awareness in your heart. I urge you to become an active participant as you expand your life. A Taoist is one with all things. There is nothing that she does not observe and apply her learning to. In order to be really happy in our everyday lives, we have to become involved. Be helpful to a stranger. Be an attentive listener to a friend. Greet every person you meet with a warm and sincere smile. These daily actions will bring a thousandfold return on your investment. Learn to extend yourself, beyond yourself. Accept all events with the understanding that they may hold both positive and negative aspects, while remembering that there is value in each for us. Seek out the Gift in every day. Use your growing wisdom to look beyond just what is in front of you. The greatest mysteries of life are well hidden. To a Taoist, they lay in plain sight.

We have learned the most important lesson in our lives; *Life is not about me.* Once we learn and accept this, the true path to happiness is revealed. How long you have searched for it! So simple, but yet so true, I assure you, it is the greatest truth you will ever know.

How you react to events will determine their impact on you. *Is there anything we can control in life except how we react to it?* Think about that statement. In the course of our lifetimes, we all will carry our share of burdens. Some are more tangible than others. In time, we learn that how we react to a given situation is really all the control we have. Many of us hide our sorrows and carry on in silence. It is the only system we have known.

"The mass of men lead lives of quiet desperation.
What is called resignation is confirmed desperation."

Henry David Thoreau

Truer words I have never read. What is Thoreau telling us here? In two simple sentences, he has summed up how most humans face their problems. By carrying on without facing or dealing with their problems, we resign ourselves to their control over us. I have met many people that fit that description in my life. I am sure you have also. In our self-examination, make sure we are not one of them.

With the use of the Tao, you will rationalize these events in proper perspective. They no longer will control you. Proper action will minimize their damaging effects. In time you will learn to use them to make yourself stronger! Remember, there are no limits to how perfect you can be. The choice is yours, it always has been. Your conscious decision to climb will change you forever. Famous songwriter John Cougar Mellencamp said it best -

"An honest man's pillow is his piece of mind."

As we live our lives, we must walk with dignity and integrity, living our lives in honor, upholding the values we claim to respect. You must want to become the image of all that you revere, and display that to the world every day, that some may find the spark and drive their own need to change.

Ask a child who their heroes are. You will hear answers like Spiderman, Luke Skywalker or Indiana Jones. These characters are all very real in our minds. They play roles of men who have conquered complex challenges, if only to entertain us. But today's real heroes are not on a cereal box. They will never be movie stars, for riches elude them. It is hard to find them; they don't wear a cape or save the world in the traditional sense. They go to work in the morning after spending another sleepless night with a dying child. They crawl to their beds with the determination of a battered fighter, getting ready for the next bell, after months of chemotherapy and radiation. They are the innocent accident victims facing a lifetime of hospitalizations and misery through no fault of their own. They endure all type of pain and suffering, and in their silence I hear their cries.

Those that rise up against these challenges, that choose not to accept the "bad things" at face value, they have changed their own reality. The situation is what it is—they know they cannot change that. But they pull together superhuman strength to make their lives valuable. They extend themselves past their own suffering to reach a world that so desperately needs their guidance, and they give themselves to it. No stuntmen, no second takes, no safety nets or stand-ins. No million dollar salaries. Not one ounce of fame or recognition. This is the real deal. They find new ways to live again. These are the heroes I see in today's world. We all have the power to be one. You just have to make the conscious choice. We really lack heroes in today's world. They haven't disappeared—they just lead quiet honorable lives like you and me.

Look deep inside your closet, is there a Superman costume waiting for you? It may surprise you. It has been my personal opinion that we possess about ten times more strength than we think we own. Usually adversity drives us to seek that costume. Though we have learned that in the concept of learning to surrender, we need to remove our costume, here is where we find its true purpose in our lives. Again we see the lesson of timing. Once found, you will become unstoppable; no obstacle will ever hold you back again! It just takes the strength to put it on.

In modern society we tend to look to popular television characters, politicians, models, and actors, even the nightly news people or talk show hosts as some pseudo hero persona. We rely too heavily on the media for our information and our entertainment. It is fine to use these mediums, just don't use them exclusively for our role models. Our children tend to be easily influenced by these representations, and some adults as well I suspect. Our real role models are seldom found in print at all. They have the scars to show you of their genuine battles. They are too humble to accept recognition. They do the best they can with what they have, and collapse in their beds every night, appreciable to enter slumber's welcome arms, that tomorrow always holds the promise of a better day. Do you recognize any Taoist qualities here? They have made the choice to make the most of what life brings to them, with no reservations, and with open arms to whomever they meet.

When we rest our head on our pillow for the very last time, let all remember us as the peaceful hero that the Tao has taught us to be. Your inspiration will change the world.

> "Those who know do not talk. Those who talk do not know."
>
> *Lao Tzu*

Here we read once again the infinite wisdom from Lao Tzu. It explains in simple yet paradoxical words why the wisdom of life and all of its answers are so well hidden. Those that have found their truths understand that revelation comes in the form of a whisper, not a shout. In understanding the Tao, we turn down the volume of life's white noise, the clatter and the relentless din that assaults our ears, so that we can get back to basics and learn how to just be ourselves again, and learn to see and feel the simplicity of a balanced life. My wish is that this book will be the whisper that starts an avalanche within your mind.

> "All men must die, but not every man truly lives."
>
> *Unknown*

In our deeper understanding and our new view of the world within your world, we now truly *live* our lives. Upon looking back at our past views, we were literally running in place. With proper perspective, we now have begun to *experience* life instead of struggle with it as we once did. Enjoy it and take pride in your new perspective. Not many people learn this lesson in their lives. They wander aimlessly their entire existence. Live now that you may show them "The Way."

In Parting

Looking back on our journey, we have traveled far! I hope I have taken you to some places you have never known. Perspective is the mother of balance. Like the king, I hope you have learned stillness. Like the boy and the hawk, I hope that you have learned the lesson of desire. From our day on the lake, you have learned balance. From the train we have learned insight and perspective. Finally, from our baseball player, I hope you have learned to swing for the fence—every day of your life.

There are many paths up the mountain. My answers will not be your answers. With the insight of this book, I hope to have instilled in you some new ideas. I have given you the tools. I have given you direction. Now you must do the work. It is all up to you.

> "People take different roads seeking fulfillment and happiness. Just because they're not on your road doesn't mean they've gotten lost."
>
> *H Jackson Brown Jr.*

Do you still believe in coincidences? Perhaps, just maybe, do you feel that there might be a cosmic force that supplies us what we need, when we need it? All we have to do is look for it and use what it supplies to us. Is it also a coincidence that of all the millions of books in the world, this one has come to you at this time in your life?

From this very day forward, you will see the world through different eyes. Has it changed, or just your perception of it? Our perceptions become our realities. In my journeys, I have learned many things. They have taken me to many places; some dark and foreboding, some so beautiful, they defy description. But in the end, it has been my choices that have led me to my path.

> "Two paths diverged in a wood, and I took the one less traveled. And that has made all the difference."
>
> *Robert Frost*

The light of the open mind and the open heart illuminate all darkness. In this place, your seeds will flourish in a beauty far beyond the tangled brush of common man. May you one day share your own Eden, and inspire a world which so desperately needs your guidance. From the student you will one day become the teacher. From the teacher, you may become the master. A master's humility is the soil that enriches the Earth and brings all to their fruition. As we leave my garden, you now pass back into your own world. Looking back, take what you have found into your own garden, and begin your own Eden. In time, we may pass this gift to many others and one day, just perhaps, it will cover the Earth. I can't wait for Heaven—I'm building it right here, right now.

The spirit of the Tao has carried me through it all, not just surviving, but also thriving beyond all imagination in a state of happiness I find difficult to describe. I want this for you my friend. With no fear in life or in death, or what tomorrow brings, I walk in serenity among the Gods. Take these lessons to heart. Reshape your world today with the faith that success and daily happiness all lie waiting for you. Your heart will show you the way. I will know when our eyes meet, that you have joined me in our walk through Eden. If you see me dancing in the rain, you will know that I am not crazy, just connected to it all. Come join me, I promise you it will be a dance you will never forget.

Thanks for walking with me. Someday we may meet, and pass through each other's houses. If not, we will certainly feel each other in the whirlpool. I see you on the mountain. Be patient in your climb, do it any way you can, but most of all, begin. The journey has begun. The spiritual path is unveiled. Your life is waiting for you, farther up the mountain.

A Message for the Reader

In these pages, I have lured you, ever so delicately through my book. I find that quotes from life's great authors to be timeless and pointed. They give an acute perspective to the reader in their brief but intense messages. The poems I wrote were to express in yet another form, feelings and perspective that can only be gained by this format, a window into my mind. My goal was one of awareness. I wanted ever so much to take you to the highest mountain and suddenly remove the blindfold that has prevented you from seeing what you have been missing.

This book was written solely for you. Having never written before, it was a challenge to create. I took this challenge on despite the overwhelming number of adversities and tasks that I have been given in this life to own. It is my sincerest commitment to your happiness and an intense mission in my soul for your own personal contentment that has driven these words upon the pages. Though you may not accept all that was here, I have provided many of life's keys for you to take. I urge you to unlock some of your doors that have held you back. If you take one key, let it change your life. It was meant for you. In the great cycle of life, the universe and all that is, the message here has washed upon your shore, a gift from me to you.

Sincerely,

JR

Appendix

Because ancient Chinese text is very subjective when translated into English, many versions exist of the Tao Te Ching. Below I have included two of my favorites. In this book I have included several of my own translation. While a literal conversion reads very broken, I have intended always to convey the spirit of Taoism into modern times that this ageless world may pass from Lao Tzu to you transferable, tangible and pure.

If the writings of Lao Tzu are the symphony of understanding, then the music lives in the sound, that the musician merely plays, to traverse generations, and arrives as if anew.

Additional recommended reading material -

Jonathan Livingston Seagull	Richard Bach	**ISBN:** 0380012863
Tao of Pooh	Benjamin Hoff	**ISBN:** 0140067477
Tao Te Ching	Gis-Fu Feng (Translator)	**ISBN:** 0679776192
Tao Te Ching	Stephen Mitchell (Translator)	**ISBN:** 0060812451
Everyday Tao	Deng Ming-Dao	**ISBN:** 0062513958
Entering the Tao	Hua-Ching Ni	**ISBN:** 1570621616
Mutant Message Down Under	Marlo Morgan	**ISBN:** 0060926317
Walden and Civil Disobedience	Henry David Thoreau	**ISBN:** 0451527070
Nature and Walking	Henry David Thoreau	**ISBN:** 0807014192

A note on Thoreau –

Henry David Thoreau is well recognized as a very deep and thoughtful writer, but his works can be difficult to translate into our modern times and verbiage. While it can be complex for the reader at first, a continued persistence is well worth the effort. There is a depth in his mind, which is sadly missing in modern times. I encourage you to draw from that well for yourself. I have found it refreshment for a lifetime...

About the Author

Joseph Roggenbeck is a forty-four year old Quality Engineer working for a major auto company living in a small town in Michigan. Here he and his wife Cindy have raised their two grown daughters Jennifer and Michelle.

He studies ancient Chinese art and philosophy in his spare time as well as music, gardening and writing poetry. His love of nature and a deep understanding of the human condition are the result of an intense life long search in learning ways to apply Taoism into a modern day Western world. As a student, he is relentless in his search for inner perfection. As a teacher he asks that you judge yourself, in his story now written.

Printed in the United States
24109LVS00001B/308